TOO MUCH POWER

When power and greed collude, justice falters

Mr. Richard A. Whalen

WORKBOOK PRESS LLC
187 E Warm Springs Rd,
Suite B285, Las Vegas, NV 89119, USA

Website: https://workbookpress.com/
Hotline: 1-888-818-4856
Email: admin@workbookpress.com

Ordering Information:
Quantity sales. Special discounts are available on quantity purchases by corporations, associations, and others.
For details, contact the publisher at the address above.

Library of Congress Control Number:
ISBN-13:   978-1-957618-60-9 (Paperback Version)
                978-1-957618-61-6 (Digital Version)

REV. DATE: 02/08/2022

TOO MUCH POWER

WHEN POWER AND GREED COLLUDE, JUSTICE FALTERS

RICHARD A. WHALEN

TABLE OF CONTENTS

"UT PROSIM" (That I May Serve) are the letters engraved into the crest of Virginia Polytechnic Institute and State University. These words meant little to me while at college other than I would go into the service and serve my country, be courteous, kind and fair with my dealings with other people. I wore the crest of Virginia Tech daily with these words emblazoned into the crest on my military uniform cap. I really didn't think much about it, in a military college you are expected to do more. Today the words ring loud and clear. It is not graduating and getting the best paying job you can, sending in Alumni donations that make you a good alum or sitting on one of your child's Parent Teachers Association committees. It's not about what you learned in college.

It is about being from a respected military college and having the training necessary to go out in the world and do anything right. It is about doing the right thing by others inreaching out to help those who cannot help themselves. Putting yourself on the line when the chips are down and the night is at its darkest. When there is nobody to help you make the right choices when you see the consequences in front of you. When it is easier to back down and do nothing, you go forward.

I can only think and wonder about those who served and didn't come back, for they sacrificed far more than I did. Only, I lived to tell about it. Or did I?

This book does not hold back any punches. Good, bad or indifferent I am telling it as it was, as I lived it, as I suffered through it and all that it took for me to get there to begin with. I didn't change any names as the innocent have nothing to worry about, but I do not have all the names of the players at the time of this writing. Exact words spoken from 30 years ago are fuzzy, but the meaning is loud and clear.

This book is dedicated to:

Those who stand up against injustice

Chapter 1:

THINGS HAPPEN

Have you ever walked a dark lonely street at night and felt something strange would happen if you turned left instead of right, or had the hair on the nape of your neck bristle outward with anticipation that someone or something bad was going to happen if you stopped? You just know a set of unfriendly eyes are set upon, but you see no one, you hear nothing and yet you are certain something is going to grab you.

Have you ever sensed the presence of somebody you have had a connection with is near? Or that someone has a feeling of ill will towards you? Maybe so, but is it energy being emanated from that person that you have the ability to pick up, or is it coincidence or maybe just superstition?

On the other hand, have you ever met someone and felt an evil or unsettling presence when they are near? No matter how pleasant the meeting is, the feeling becomes over-powering and you just want to get away.

All of these feelings have come over me at one time or another. So many choices occur in one's life that can completely change you forever or leave you in a status quo. Some call it fate, others a guiding hand helping one thru life. But, I have had more than my share of life changing incidents. Here is my story and these happenings did occur to me. This is my story of events that happened between 1975 and 1985.

I had come back to the southwestern Virginia where I had gone to college and met my wife. She had strong family ties there and I loved the mountains. While living on the coastal flatlands and on Long Island, there were no mountains. I missed the mountains in the background, strong unwavering sentinels. I missed the fresh air that didn't get fouled up with exhaust gasses from vehicles, industry and power plants. What I didn't miss were the traffic jams, congestion, crowds, shopping lines, toll booth lines and crowded parking lots. It is not that I didn't like people, just being hassled by too many people. Maybe I was a little claustrophobic too. When I would look over the horizon, all I could see was smog.

The first year we got settled into our new southern lives. We got involved with a local faith group in Floyd, Virginia and went to church regularly Sunday and some Wednesday nights. The job was ok, work was easy and no pressure so we decided to built our house starting next spring on the property.

CHAPTER 2:

DAY ONE

I remember that fateful late summer afternoon well. There was a light breeze blowing from the west and the temperature was in the low nineties. I was on the roof of my new ranch home, the foundation and framing just completed. I was working on weekends finishing the roofing, setting shingles along the blue snap line that I and a helper snapped on the previous weekend when we put the rolled asphalt underlayment down. I was sweating a lot and remember the cooling breeze that swept over my head every time I sat up for a new batch of shingles. It would send chills all over my body. My wife, Ginny was watching our 2 young boys, Richard Jr. and Michael. They would be scurrying around the house playing with left over building materials and throwing gravel at each other. Ginny's job was to refill my cup of roofing nails and bring me something to drink as I needed them.

I loved it on the roof, one could almost see forever as the house stood at the top of the rim of a small stream valley to the south and east and a large flat farming area to the west. The drop off down the valley continued for about 5 miles to the main road into Floyd from Roanoke, Virginia. It then rose up for 3 miles beyond to the prominent Haycocks, a small group of sugarplum hilltops along the Blue Ridge Parkway, then to the escarpment where it dropped down to the Piedmont. On a clear day I could see all the way to Flattop Mountain in North Carolina from my perch atop the house. But was not visible from the ground level. The view was outstanding and I could only see 4 houses along the dirt road from our house. I could see most of the 97-acre farm from the house as about a half of it was on the other side of the stream below rising to the top of the next hill beyond running into a wooded area and disappearing from sight.

While hammering down shingle after shingle, a somewhat over used light pinkish colored station wagon pulled into our driveway and stops at the pile of as of yet unused interior framing materials. Out of the car came a small statured almost frail red headed young man, 2 young redheaded children and a very pregnant wife stepped out taking her time getting their 3rd child, and as of then, youngest child from the rear baby seat. He walked up to the house and called me down from the roof. He was one of the local church congregation members that my wife and I had not yet met. My kids were playing in the dirt along the driveway and their kids eagerly joined in. Meanwhile my wife was getting ready to have a late lunch. He had a slight but pronounced New England accent. But, as it turned out he was the county solicitor just recently passed the bar exam. This was his first job as an attorney in Virginia. He brought his wife and children to help make the visit seem more cordial. I sat down on a pile of 2 by 4 framing lumber which made a good seat and picnic table where we properly introduced ourselves. After some niceties he began to come to the reason he stopped by.

He heard I was an Engineer. "Yes, a Civil Engineer graduate of Virginia Tech class of '66" I responded. He had been the county solicitor for about 6 months and was still getting to know his way about Floyd County. He stated he wasn't here on official business.

But, he was also the attorney representing the Citizens for the Preservation of Floyd County. This was a private and hastily organized group of local farmers and property owners with no expertise and / or engineering experience. The citizens group was holding a meeting at the courthouse next Monday in downtown Floyd and he begged me to come to it. Well, not really begged, but pleaded to my better sense of citizenship.

This was a group of unrepresented citizens that needed someone with engineering expertise to represent them to help mount a fight against a power line proposed by Appalachian Power Company traversing right thru the middle of Floyd County. As it turned out this was no ordinary power line. The group knew they could not fight it without some real engineering help, they had tried to get others experienced with these matters to help, but nobody wanted to fight the power company.

This was a mammoth 765 Kva power line. That was 765,000 volts and it was the biggest of all power lines built in America. It was being sponsored by the parent company of Appalachian Power, American Electric Power Company. They were probably the most powerful publicly owned Power Company in America. I looked at my family, showed him my just framed house and told him I didn't want to get involved at this time. My time was limited between my job and working on the house. But he begged me saying I was only needed as a token engineer to represent the group and give the group some credibility. We talked a little more, but I still didn't give an answer. We shook hands and one last please help us before parting. I climbed back on the roof as they pulled away onto the dirt road and a trail of dust following behind them until they disappeared over the next rise. My stomach was now filled with a picnic lunch and now I had new things in my head to think about. Ginny and the boys walked down the side of the hill and began picking huckleberries that grew wild on the southeast facing slope. They were tiny blueberries that had 5 times the taste of store bought blueberries and would soon become one of my favorite fall and winter home-made pies.

CHAPTER 3:

NOTHING BUT HOPE

I broke down and went to that Monday night meeting. Maybe it was just out of curiosity, or maybe some other force was guiding me there. I went alone as Ginny stayed home tending to the boys. The courthouse was packed with farmers and residents of all ages. All the seats were taken and some people were standing in the rear and along the sides of the courtroom. They quietly milled around and whispered to each other expecting something to happen. As the meeting started, a hush came over the room only to be broken by a late comer gently closing the door behind him. The county solicitor began to speak about the upcoming hearings with the State Corporation Commission, the date of which was not yet set. He then introduced me as the one man that would design a new power line route that would not pass thru Floyd County at all. They all applauded and I hadn't even accepted the job yet. I wasn't told that was what I was going to do and I just sat there listening to the proceedings.

They had nothing else but hope. How could I refuse a little help for these desperately deserving and yet unknowing people? Did I even have the expertise to take on this challenge? I have never even worked on anything remotely similar to this. I wasn't an Electrical Engineer. Thoughts like "I don't know if I can do this, why should I try this if I don't know what to do" and "can I possibly succeed in this endeavor?" ran through me. Eventually I changed my mind to "I'm sure I can do it!, maybe."

At the end of the meeting many came to shake my hand and thank me for helping them. Now I knew what my job was to be and I had a good sense of what was needed to do it.

Of course one of the tasks of the group was to get as many members of Floyd County to sign up with a donation of $5.00 to help defray costs. I specifically said I didn't want to be a member to the Citizens for the Preservation of Floyd County, just utilize me as an unpaid advisor. I didn't want anybody to make an inference that I was hired by the group. At the end of the meeting the solicitor went into his office and gave me a handful of filings and the proposed routings that the State Corporation Commission was reviewing from Appalachian Power Company. I found out that for all the other counties the power line ran thru, Floyd was the only county to file as Protestants and he, as the county solicitor, would represent both the group and the county supervisors. The Floyd County Board of Supervisors also opposed the power line by official resolution. On my way out a number of citizen farmers shook my hand some more a told me they knew I would do a good job for them. The weight of this project was now clearly on my shoulders. The county solicitor just got off the hook. He had successfully passed the buck, the main work load, onto someone else. I would only get to speak with him a few more times before the important State Corporation Commission meeting which was being scheduled to be held in Floyd County regarding the proposed location of the power line.

CHAPTER 4:

THE TASK AT HAND

Well, what is there to do? I now had been working for the Roanoke County Department of Public Works as the County Engineer for about a year. Art Guepe was my direct superior and the Director of Public Works. There was only one step above him and that was the County Administrator, Mr. William F. Clark. As a dutiful employee I had constantly informed Art about my off hours' involvement in the citizens group from day 1 and he fully supported it. He always had a smile on his face and was eager to hear about events that happened along the way. Art was always easy for me to work with and talk to as he too was an engineer being a graduate of Vanderbilt University, about 4 or 5years ahead of me.

I read through the documents supplied by Appalachian Power Company during the late summer nights as we completed the house. I guess I was lucky being the county engineer as the electrical and plumbing inspectors for Roanoke County came to the house and gave me some help and very useful advice along the way like using 12-2 with ground wiring instead of 14-2 with ground wiring which was the common household standard for that time period. That was a slightly thicker copper wire than the standard wire and would help maintain better electrical flow thru the house. I always offered to pay them each time they came out, but a few cold old beers and a laugh or 2 was all they needed.

Skilled help was difficult to find out here. I did manage to find a local out of work jack of all trades who was willing to help for bottom dollar on the weekends. Sometimes he even came out just to talk, and talk, and talk. I learned a lot about the area from him, he was a 30-year-old out of work mason assistant and ended up talking me into letting him do the outside brick work.

Hanging the drywall in 12 foot lengths from the ceiling was the most difficult job for Ginny and me. I would jamb one end into the ceiling wall edge and she came in and pushed it up with a "T" pole to secure it against the rafters. Then I lifted it up more and another pole pushed in and finally we both pushed up the end. Then I got to do my work, hammering in drywall nails from underneath. What a job that was. The heating system was the last to go in before we got the final occupancy inspection from the county building inspector.

We moved in that fall just before winter set in. During this time in our new ranch home I had already read the proposed route and the massive report made by Virginia Tech on the environmental effects of the power line and its location. They were using a new computer technology that was able to find 2 separate and distinct routes of least resistance thru the environmentally sensitive Blue Ridge mountain and valley complex. The entire area was divided into grids of about ½ mile squares and field surveys were made by graduate students identifying all flora, fauna and other environmental properties of each box, then assigning a weighted number to each critical area of each box. The site was chosen by adding all the critical areas in all the boxes the line went thru and the 2 possible routes that had the least total number were chosen.

The proposed line ran from a power substation along the existing east - west 765 Kva power line that ran from east of the Mississippi River area to Lynchburg Virginia. It met another 500 Kva power line coming up from the Carolina Power and Light in Wythe/Pulaski County area to the west of us at the existing Jackson's Ferry Power Substation. This existing 765 Kva substation was the starting point of the 2 proposed lines. They then ran southeastward into Floyd County, then down the Blue Ridge Mountain escarpment to meet with a substation in Martinsville, Virginia. The proposed line then was to meet an existing 500 Kva power line going down to Carolina Power and Light. This was the northern end of their 500 Kva power line system coming up from the south and east from us. Power coming into Virginia from this station was only being transmitted by local 138 Kva lines running up to the Roanoke area. Both proposed 765 Kva lines cut thru the heart of Floyd County. These proposed routes have more mileage running thru open farmland and homesteads in Floyd County than any other county along its proposed path, which were mostly heavily wooded areas.

One line went south of the town of Floyd and the other north of the town of Floyd. I found during the plotting of these lines that the northern route was to run right past my farm. Of course that wasn't a reason to fight this line as it was a totally safe and harmless to humans and animals alike according to the power company. I didn't even tell my wife that the north route was running thru our farm, as I didn't want the emotions of the landowners to take away from my focusing on the subject at hand. I went to the engineering store and purchased a complete set of United States Geographical Survey (USGS) topographic maps for all possible routings. I had to go back to the map store many times as I kept expanding the reach of the outside bounds, not knowing exactly were the placement would be and how far I wandered away from the 2 proposed routes. The pace picked up as there was a pre-thanksgiving town meeting with the citizens group and they wanted to hear about what I was doing. There was no magical bolt of lightning showing me the way. Using the restraints placed upon the Virginia Tech design team, the results would always come out the same, the shorter the line, the less ecological damage. The real problem was nobody was thinking out of the box. Floyd County was the box.

CHAPTER 5:

CIVILIAN LIFE

There was no parade or gratitude of thanks for serving our country, just an honorable discharge, which I got about 6 months after I was mustered out and the all-important DD-214 eligibility paper which entitled me to G.I. benefits. I was lucky as it didn't take me but a few weeks to get a good job as a facilities engineer for a branch of the New York Telephone Company. My first 6 months were getting familiar with the work. My boss, Eddy, was the company's managing engineer. He was impressed with my work and quickly promoted me to a full line after my 6 months' probation period.

Shortly after I was given an in line promotion to a new and more responsible position. That was the position of a recently retired 2nd line facilities engineer. I was told that it was company policy to give the line grade promotion if I were to perform the duties well for 1 full year. My duties were to schedule and oversee the all the construction crews' in Manhattan and the Bronx. I did very well in this position, but it required that I needed to work 60+ hour weeks as many important projects in Manhattan could only be done on weekends and at night. During this time my wife, Virginia gave me my first born, a son, Richard Jr. But, the work continued to increase and home life was minimal. The only time I remember spending with my wife was going to our favorite Chinese restaurant with Richie in a safety seat next to us in a booth. On my first anniversary I was officially given this position and told if I did well for the next year it would be a promotion to 2ⁿᵈ line. This meant that I now had full authority and responsibility for 60 company employees. My job was to keep them working in a continuous flow of work plus keeping track of some outside contractors when needed.

After the birth of my son Richie, one of the contract engineers hired by outside consulting firms due to excessive construction of underground telephone conduits had to leave the job. At that time there was nobody else experienced enough to take over at such short notice. I was pushed out there to take his place until he returned. I still had my other duties to perform. This job was located on one of the major avenues of New York City and could only be opened up and worked on the weekends. One Saturday afternoon the owner of the construction company visited the job site. This was an Italian heritage owned company and in New York City, that meant only one thing, the mob was behind it. After a quick lunch at a local sidewalk restaurant he pulled out a wad of $100 bills and told me to take a vacation for a week and his foreman would keep the daily records. He informed me that he had done this with most, if not all of the onsite contract engineer inspectors that the engineering company hired for major projects. He asked "How do you think the inspector I was replacing got to go take his family on a cruise for a week?" I flat out refused. Interestingly he was not disappointed though and said I was the first one ever to turn him down. He then stood up and threw the $1,500 on the table and said it was a gift for the birth of my son a week earlier. As he walked away he said "You don't refuse a gift from us, or it's taken as an insult". Well, there it was, $1,500 in $100 bills of real money partly uncurled from its hand rolled wad just sitting on the table staring at me. Do I take it or just leave it there? That would be one hell of a tip.

Honesty really is the best policy. But, how many other people like me in the company were taking the graft money from contractors? I was to find out next summer that one of my good friends in the company was getting an envelope full of $50 bills every week. When he went on vacation he asked me to take the envelope for him from the contractor he was working with. When I gave him the envelope, I never associated with him again at company bowling or soft ball games, ever. Neither was this to be the last time I would end up working with the mob.

After my 2nd year and the big promotion due to come which everyone including myself thought was in the bag, I got the call to the chief engineer's office. I walked in with a big smile on my face. The chief engineer started to read from the progress report. Eddy had previously gone over this evaluation with me. What he read to me sounded perfectly ok. That was until he got to the point that said that I was late to the office one morning and therefore needed more time at the office before I could get the promotion. I would need to have at least 1 more full year more before I could even be considered for that job. I was floored, where did this come from. I went to Eddie's office and spoke to him about this.

He said he highly recommended my promotion and didn't put in that part about my tardiness. He tried to tell me that these were old school engineers and they didn't work the same way we did. The chief engineer put that in himself as the only negative part of my yearly report. It hit me; the manager lived on Long Island and took the same train into Brooklyn as I did, then the same subway into Manhattan. I specifically remembered that one. The train was late because we were on it together and we both entered the building's front door at 8:45 AM together. That's how he knew I was 15 minutes late once. I worked my tail off for a year and a half to get this promotion and then its thrown out the window like a piece of junk. My new job was sitting at a desk in charge of the drafting department of which got boring fast, real fast. I was being punished for being late once. Everybody at the office knew it was a demotion. Well, I finally gave notice and left for the heavy construction side where all the action was in New York City. I never should have left, but I needed my self-esteem.

Work from there on slowed down as construction projects in the early 1970's were being postponed. During this time more and more veterans were coming home to no work at all. My new job was close to home and gave much more time with my family. I was the assistant project manager for a very large sewer interceptor project on the southern side of Long Island in Nassau County. The project manager was having a very difficult time with the project, installing a 96 inch sewer main 15 feet deep under the main road. What did I get myself into? The job was dead on arrival. He would not take any suggestions. He just stood in one place looking into the trenches trying to figure it out. I told him I would take a crew and put the lateral sewer lines in, as we would soon pass the point where the well points that drew down the ground water from the deep trench would keep the water down enough for the higher smaller lines to be installed. This worked so well and was just in time to boost the monthly billings. After 2 months of putting in thousands of feet of lateral lines and moving ahead of the main line which only moved a few hundred feet, I was laid off. Why?

But things started to look up when I signed on with Conduit & Foundation Construction Corporation. I ran a small sized project which was the installation of a 36 inch medium pressure gas line in the Bronx successfully. At the end of the project they sent me downtown to a job that was killing them financially. I was hearing numbers like $1 million in the red, and it hardly started. This project was a major building foundation project. This was for a 40-story New York Telephone building located at the northwest corner of the Brooklyn Bridge. Steel piles were being driven 80 to 200+ feet into bedrock with water pressure coming in from the East River. The job was a disaster when I got there, only 2/3 excavated and a handful of the 2,200 piles driven. Labor problems plagued the site as dock builders and pile drivers were walking off the job an hour or more early every day complaining about the working conditions.

Of course Bernie, the company general manager wouldn't go into the trenches and threw the job to me as a scapegoat to sink or swim. The previous job super was Bernie's hand-picked man who he had to let him go with extreme pressure from the top. Needless to say, once I got started, most of my time during the normal working hours was spent down in the hole with the foremen and crews. This way they couldn't complain about the conditions as long as I was down there with them. After normal work hours were over, the job required I do all the paper work that needed to be completed before I could go home. There were 3 separate pile driving crews. Two main crews were used to drive piles and the third handled the steel piles and tested the completed pile groups. We were still behind schedule. I had to do something that would get the pile driving crews producing at least 50% more and they didn't want to speak to me. I wasn't a member of their union, nor a member of any union. I was a company man. I noticed that when things were working well they could get a good pile count. But something would always seem to go wrong, like clockwork. Then they would leave the job when the mechanic got there. I knew they were intentionally fowling up the pile drivers by sitting on the piles too long causing the compression ring to give out, or causing the rigging itself to get jammed. If they could get to this point every day, why couldn't they get further.

I made a competition with the men that if they exceeded a daily minimum pile production they got to work an extra 2 hours at double time if they wanted as long as they continued to work. That meant they would have to get in 8 piles in a day which is more than their 5 piles per day they were averaging and have no more breakdowns. Plus, they could get another 2 piles per day in during the overtime which would bring the total to 10 piles per crew per day. That would be double the daily production for only 2 more hours of overtime. It was a success, even the 3rd crew was busy trying to keep up with the other 2 pile driving crews who were averaging well over 10 piles per day. They even got to work 1-hour overtime per day just testing piles just to keep up. The real cost of the job wasn't in a few hours of double time but the other 100 laborers, iron workers and concrete masons who could not stand about waiting for the piles to be driven. This is just where I wanted to be.

One of the most critical areas was the supply of piles. They were so long, these trucks were not allowed on the city streets after 6:00 am on delivery day. Trucks would be lined up around the block waiting for the early crew to get there at 6:30 am. Needless to say, I was also there. My day started with the first man on the job didn't end until my paper work was completed or until the last man left the job site.

My family life was almost non-existent. After our 2nd son, Michael was born I hardly got to see him awake. The killer experience came when Michael was about 6 months' old and I got home early. Ginny met me at the door holding Mickie high in her arms. He was frightened, turned his head into his mother's shoulders and started to cry. He didn't know who I was. Was my work so important that it should tear away at my family life? Did I need to make a change?

As the job was winding down, I had been hearing how pleased management was with the job that was now making good money and I heard about the next really big job getting ready to start and that is was a large complicated project. Just as we were setting the last of the flying forms on the last outside retaining wall, Bernie comes up to me with a friend standing behind at the trailer. He had an envelope and said I was fired. He stated I hired a relative for summer work while in college without company permission. It was my brother in-law. I had gotten full permission from Bernie that spring before bringing him on as a lowly concrete laborer. My blood pressure started to boil and I almost threw him off the catwalk 30 feet above the concrete flooring. But I didn't, he had his dock builder buddy that was out of work waiting for him back at the construction trailer. He had given him the job.

Then there was another job that I hired on to build a subway extension and station in Brooklyn. I was started with a full set of plans and I began to lay out the job. I was trying to lay out where to start and the sequence of events needed to do the job properly. But I kept looking for a tie in with the surrounding streets and buildings. There were none, they just overlaid the project onto the street map. Survey points noted on the map were not found on the ground. The boss sent it to the subway engineers and they couldn't reconcile the problem either. The project was put on hold for a year. Out of work again I began to feel I needed something simpler and more secure.

It hit me that I could never get ahead at this business as long as I was smarter than those above me. Being successful made me a threat to their position. Being smarter than my boss or superior only made it more difficult for me to speak to them. Why couldn't I seem to get ahead and always find myself looking for work after doing well. Maybe it was really the time for me to make a big change.

I began looking the engineering trade journals for possible job relocation and eventually found a position offered as a county engineer in Roanoke, Virginia, near my old stomping grounds, an area familiar to both my wife and me. I sent in my resume and was called up that week in response. We went down to Roanoke, Virginia for an interview and I spent that weekend with my wife at her aunt's place in Radford, Virginia where I had met her years earlier. I was offered the job that week. She was all for it with family and friends in the area, secure job with no overtime. We also owned a small farm in Floyd County, which abuts Roanoke County and it made some sense to try it.

Now let me tell you about Floyd County. It was lacking as many of the modern conveniences as one could imagine. Many areas didn't have electricity until the 1950's. The telephone system was Floyd citizen owned a co-op. All lines were party lines with up to 10 separate homes on each line. If you wanted to hear the latest gossip about the neighborhood, just pick up the line and listen. The hard part was clearing the line to make a real phone call. You had to pick up the phone and click on it when others were using it. Hang up, and then wait a minute for the parties to get off, then pick up again and ring the operator for an outside line. We just moved into a time warp 50 years behind the rest of civilization.

The first year we were there we got involved with a local Christian group in Floyd and went to church regularly Sunday and some Wednesday nights in Floyd. The job was ok, work was easy and no pressure to detract from family life. The group sponsored a couple's weekend encounter retreat of which we agreed to go to. This was a highly structured weekend focusing on our getting to know each other again. Realizing that we had drifted apart, we concentrated on getting to be more in touch with each other.

Chapter 6:

THE NEW LINES

The power company was disseminating information about how safe the 765 Kva lines were and totally innocuous to the communities they passed through. My wife and I went on a field trip put on by the citizens group one evening just as the sun set behind the hills to the west. We boarded an old school bus with about 30 other people. Driving thru the dimly lit twilight, I could not recognize where I was. We pulled onto a farm about 30 miles from Floyd where an existing 765 Kva line ran thru in adjacent Pulaski County.

We got off the bus and everybody was handed a long florescent light bulb. We all walked towards the power line about 100 yards away. Just as we got within 50 feet of the line, the light bulbs began to glow, the closer we came, the brighter they became and you could feel this funny little tingling in your hand. The electromagnetic field generated by the power line was causing electrons to flow thru our bodies into the light tubes. But that wasn't the only thing I noticed about the power line, there was a consistent low-level hum being generated by the transmission lines. During the following weeks I became more aware of the power lines and how they cut through farmlands and across mountains. The most noticeable of these was along I-81 in Roanoke County running over the mountain directly north of I-81 and at very shallow angle. This scar made by this line was visible from just about everywhere in the Roanoke Valley. One foggy morning I was driving slowly through a quiet farming valley with my window down, my window is always down except during the worst of weather. The fog was hanging about 20 feet above the ground and I had little visibility beyond that. I could see the fences on both sides of the road and somewhat into the fields that slowly vanished into a grey soup. I began hearing noises like a snap, crackle and popping. As I slowly drove on, it got louder and louder to a point where it was distracting. Then the existing 765 Kva line appeared draping across the road almost parallel to it. After I went under and passed by it the noise dissipated. "That's not right," I thought to myself, if something like this were by my house I wouldn't be able to sleep. I began to compile as much first-hand information about these lines as I could. I noticed how the power lines ran in straight lines thru the mountains and could follow them on the topographic maps. Most lines are visible for 20 or more miles. They are so prominent that they are major visual sighting points for pilots flying VFR – visual flight rules. I started making notes and began to formulate a plan for locating new power lines. The power company had its own construction manual on how to locate power lines as I knew I had to counter with my own set of common sense rules. Then, design my new routes bypassing Floyd County altogether using the new set of rules I developed. It may sound simple, but it consumed all my extra time.

The pace was picking up in late 1975 and from here out the dates become important. I plotted the power company routes on the maps and used colored dash stickers for each proposed power line route. In order to fight the power company, you need to have a viable alternative and it became vividly apparent that the power company knew this too.

The reason for two separate lines was a divisive trick used by the ancient Romans, divide and conquer. It was supposed to create a situation where all the protestors living along the corridor passing south of the Town of Floyd would be chanting for the line to go north of the Town Floyd and on the other hand, those living along the northern line would be shouting to have the line go to south of the Town of Floyd. It worked so very well in the past that the power company must have thought it was in the bag. At the first meeting I attended there were two representatives from the power company that the solicitor pointed out to me, they were at every public meeting from day one just to report back all the group's activities to headquarters and make sure that confusion prevailed.

The next scheduled town meeting was about 1 month later. I hurried to complete the mapping of my proposed lines so I could present them to the citizens of Floyd County. When I pulled off the cover sheet from over the maps at that nights meeting, the large piece of plywood I used had maps sticking out every where along the edges, but they were surprised to see 4 separately colored and distinct lines running from the Wythe County starting point to the tie-in with Carolina Power and Light just outside Martinsville, Virginia. I had created 2 separate lines that didn't go thru Floyd County. Two because the power company presented two lines. I knew this was grasping at straws. One line ran thru the Meadows of Dan to the south of Floyd County and the other ran north of Floyd County right through Roanoke County. Yes, I did tell Art, my supervisor, which only got an approving eyebrow raised while smoking his pipe.

Other meetings were scheduled, the next one was in early January in Franklin County to the south of Floyd County. By this time my maps were more presentable, but the routing had not changed. All routes dipped down thru Franklin County on their way to the common terminus of this line.

This time the meeting was held at the Franklin County high school auditorium and had a much larger crowd there. This included many members from both Franklin County and Floyd County living along the proposed routes along with some of our citizens group and members of the press. This was an unruly group with no direction. I felt very uncomfortable as the protesting citizens of Franklin County were much more belligerent than the Floyd County group. Noise continued throughout the meeting, not the attentive yearning quietness as we had in the Floyd County Court House. There were 3 members representatives of the power company present at the meeting. They were pointed out to me by out attorney as hissing and booing followed them to their seats. Plus, this was the first time the press covered the story this time. I didn't say much of anything at that weekend meeting. I just sat on the stage and acknowledged my name as the engineer working on this project. My maps were propped up at one end of the stage for all to see. But, for the people of Franklin County there was no relief as the shorter of my proposed lines ran through the central area of Franklin County mostly thru uninhabited low lying drainage areas and unpopulated areas. There was a period of time when the attendees could speak, and just as the power company had planned, the citizens were shouting that the lines go anywhere else than on their land. Divided and conquerable.

Well, next Monday morning it made headlines, Roanoke County Engineer is "Environmental Activist" leading fight against power line. Nothing there was close to the truth. I wasn't an environmental activist and I wasn't working as the official engineer for Roanoke County with an interest in helping these people for Roanoke County, and I wasn't the leader of the group. It just made good press. What kind of interest could it generate if somebody from somewhere did something. In the late 1960's into the early 1970's when American Electric Power first tried to build these super-sized lines, environmentalists held mass meetings opposing these lines. These groups were led by scientists and protagonists that brought the fight against the power lines countrywide. And that made great press that went on and on. It also made many citizens side with the power company as the press got bitter. They eventually lost their fight and the power lines were built. Now they were trying to make me out to be one of those disrupting activists. I was none of that.

Art Guepe brought me into his office that morning to discuss these points. I flatly denied that I made any representations as the official engineer for Roanoke County. It was never mentioned at the meeting where I worked or what I was doing there other than my being a consultant to the group. So, someone was there stirring the pot and I had a good idea whom that was.

Later that day I passed Mr. Clark in the hallway and sensed something strange. I didn't know what it was, but it was there. From that day on I realized something dark was going on outside the arena where I lived and worked. Something that I should be very afraid of.

Chapter 7:

THE PLAN UNFOLDS

Constantly pouring over the maps I knew I was missing something. I needed something better. My southern route was actually ½ mile shorter than the 72 miles long shortest route proposed by the power company, but it ran thru the environmentally sensitive Meadows of Dan area. My northern route was well over 80 miles long giving no savings, it just gave the citizens group an extra hat or two to throw into the pot, but it ran right through Roanoke County where I worked, and I didn't want to stir up problems where none existed before. There had to be a better answer and I was determined to find it.

Thank God for faith groups. One of the members of a sister faith group heard about what was happening and he offered his services knowing I was looking for a pilot. He was the chief surgeon at the Christiansburg Hospital and had a 4-seat single engine plane sitting at the Blacksburg airport. I told him that I would really like to fly over the proposed lines to better get a bird's eye view so I could make adjustments. Looking at flat topography maps is nothing like the real thing. We set out that next Saturday morning flying along my southern route from the exiting substation near the Wythe, Pulaski and the Carroll County border and returning along the power company's southern route. Coming back up the northern leg I noticed there was not much different between the two lines, theirs and my shortest route.

I realized I had made up a new criteria for placing power lines and I watched how one of my new lines saved the scars on the landscape that would accompany their new power lines. Upon returning back to the starting point I asked the good doctor to follow the existing 765 Kva power line to its other end point near Lynchburg, Virginia. During this application for the new power line, Appalachian Power Company stated that another power line would be necessary and its application for construction was to follow after these hearings were completed. The second leg was to begin construction once the first leg was completed to Martinsville. It was going to go from Martinsville to Lynchburg coming back to the existing line at the Lynchburg terminus. This didn't provide more power, just a higher degree of reliability.

What we were flying over was mostly mountainous land with some farms along the flatter areas and rivers. We flew over the mountain following the long scar the 765 Kva left coming down the side of the mountain way down to the base where we found Matt Funk standing alone, by itself surrounded by woods.

Matt Funk was the name of a large substation south of Salem, Virginia that took a 275 Kva line from the Mountaineer 1 and 2 generating stations owned by Appalachian Power company that produced power from coal mined from massive coal mines owned by Appalachian Power Company. These lines came in directly in from the West Virginia generation stations and this substation had 138 Kva lines going into Roanoke from the west side feeding Roanoke County, Salem City and parts of Roanoke City. Roanoke City also had 2 sets of 138 Kva power lines feeding it 51 miles from Martinsville directly to the south. The 138 Kva line is the normal sized feeder line one sees running through and to towns suspended on tall towers with 3 arms on either side along with 3 sets of single lines suspended from arms on either side.

As we approached the substation I specifically noticed a large cleared area, larger than the existing pad for the substation serving smaller lines adjacent substation at Matt Funk's location. It sat almost adjacent to the existing station almost abutting its side. The 765 Kva line did not go to Matt Funk, but passed directly over Matt Funk, directly over the newly cleared area. Large enough for a new 765 Kva substation. It was as if they were going to build a substation for another 765 Kva line already planned by Appalachian Power Company of which they had not divulged to anyone in this hearing including the State Corporate Commission. I got the pilot's attention and pointed to go south following the existing 138 Kva power lines. And follow them we did. Then we went right to the terminus substation with the existing 500 Kva power line running straight up from Carolina Power and Light and ran directly into South Carolina.

Most of the power corridor was already there, environmental areas already breached, utility line scars already existed and almost no more damage to the environment would be done if the line were to run from the Matt Funk substation south to the Martinsville terminus. If this new 765 Kva tie in was made, it could become a new starting point to Martinsville, Virginia. Appalachian Power Company didn't need do an extensive environmental impact study to get permission to tie into the existing 765 Kva line at Matt Funk, as it didn't impact any other property that it didn't own already. Wow, did that light bulb shine brightly and none too soon as I was to find out.

After we finished our discovery flight to Martinsburg, I asked if I could take the yoke and fly a little. It was over 5 years since I last flew a plane while at Virginia Tech. He was happy to let me. Boy, did it feel good. His plane was heavier and had more power than the light training plane I was used to flying. It didn't bounce all over the place like a small 2 seat plane. Like the one I did my ROTC flight training at Virginia Tech.

I really wanted to become a pilot since I was a child. I enrolled in the Air Force R.O.T.C. program while at Virginia Tech. My senior year I got to fly a small 2-seat airplane. I was cleared to solo after just 2.5 hours of flying time. It was as if flying was second nature to me. After 7 hours of flight training my instructor decided to let me fly cross-country alone, being the earliest he ever let a student go flying cross-country alone. What a challenge that day held for me. The first leg was flying into Beckley, West Virginia, snuggled in between mountains that were just waiting to eat up small aircraft. I learned quickly that flying over mountains while into a strong headwind, the downdraft was trying so hard to smash the plane into the side of the mountains. The first mountain I came to I had to put full power on, pull the yoke back and point the plane upward. I was still descending at over 1,500 feet per minute towards the steep mountainside. That is all the rate of climb gage went to. I was flying solo and had nobody to help me make the decisions that I needed to make just to stay alive. I made up my mind that I would turn back in 30 seconds if the plane was still losing altitude and still being pushed into the mountain. I saw the mountains crest in front of me getting closer and closer. The trees that were blurred into one mass of green became individual trees. I was getting too close, I needed to turn now or crash into the mountain. I started to begin my escape turn when, suddenly I was thrust skyward at a rate of over 2,000 feet per minute. I turned the power all the way down so the propellers were just pinwheeling and I pushed the nose of the plane pointing down, way down, as far down as I could get it pointing down. The plane and I continued rising all the way up to almost 10,000 feet before the same thing happened over and over again until I finally reached Beckley. It was definitely a roller coaster ride with the first mountain being the roughest as it was the tallest. I had heard so many stories about crashes at the Beckley airport, but that flight made the landing at Beckley seem like a piece of cake.

The second leg was the long one flying into Charlottesville, Virginia. I had to cross over the same mountains again, but with the wind to my back and a little higher elevation that reduced these drastic effects. It was a long lonely flight with me looking at the scenery and checking for predominate check points along the way which included observing power line scars that showed up on my flight maps as they were highly visible from the airplane.

Only occasional chatter on the radio, but it didn't concern me. I was flying alone, solo. Then, as I was on my final approach into the Charlottesville airport I got a call from the control tower that there was passenger liner passing me on the left. I looked and didn't see anything. I kept on checking, still nothing. Suddenly, no more than a few hundred feet from my left wing appeared a propeller Martin 404 that blew by me like I was standing still. It looked as if it was only a few feet off my left wing, but telling distances suspended in air is difficult, so no more than a hundred feet or so.

That was interesting. When I left Charlottesville on my last leg home I was about an hour behind my flight schedule approaching Roanoke air space, probably due to the reduced speed facing high headwinds during my westward portions of the flight. Bad weather was moving in and I could see large storm clouds 30 miles in front of me over the mountains and they were right where I was heading.

The Blacksburg tower and my instructor were trying to get me on the radio, but I hadn't yet switched to the field's frequency as I was just leaving the Roanoke airfield area. They got me thru the Roanoke airport and stressed that I should turn around if I felt uncomfortable as cross winds were rising to 45+ MPH at Blacksburg. I continued bucking stronger and stronger head winds and cross winds as the thunderstorm had fully formed a short distance in front of me. I could see the field from outside the Christiansburg area coming over the crest of the plateau. My instructor was on the radio stressing I couldn't land if the storm got to the field. I would have to return to the Roanoke airfield. I lined up my approach and crabbed the plane to Blacksburg's only runway that was perpendicular to the winds as the windsock was indicating and fully extended. I put my flaps down and gave it more power to compensate for the strong winds. I fought as hard as I could keeping the plane heading straight to the airport while crossing the main road into Blacksburg. The wind was coming directly in from the my left to right. I pulled back on the yoke and hit the ailerons and rudder so the plane was tilting heavily to the left and landed on just 1 wheel, cut the power and kept the right wing suspended above the runway until it had no more lift and fell onto the runway leveling the plane off. When I parked the aircraft, my instructor stated he had never seen such a good crosswind landing from a student in his life. He was probably exaggerating from relief that I didn't damage the plane which could have easily flipped over. Flying solo, I did it all by myself with no outside help. After the successful cross-country flight I got to wear my wings, which I wore proudly on my uniform for the rest of my stay at Virginia Tech.

CHAPTER 8:

GET TO WORK

I got the call a week later that the attorneys for the power company had called the solicitor, or should I say county attorney. He liked to be called solicitor. They said they needed a complete copy of my testimony as the State Corporation Commission was going to hold a special fact finding hearing at the Floyd County Courthouse on March 16th 1976. This had to be done so the power company could have full disclosure of my work prior to that meeting. I frantically started to dictate my routes into a recorder. Another volunteer would pick it up from my house and type it up and give me a copy a day or two later when she came and got the next recording. This went on for about 2 weeks. First there was the fifty plus page recital as to the reasoning and criteria I developed for rerouting the power company routes out of Floyd County. One of my eleven criteria was to limit scaring of mountain sides by crossing as close to 90 degrees to the line along the mountain crest and in a very short distance turn right or left and follow the lower slopes of the mountain side between 10 and 15 degrees slope where the farm tractors can't plow and only open fields exist. This will yield virtually no scarring or minimal scaring. This portion took well over a week to complete alone. When I finished the 2 new proposed routes starting from Wythe County substation I talked to the solicitor about my new routing. I had not spoken to anyone about this as it was just formulated. No one else knew about this, not even the solicitor. The route of "no route" as I called it from Roanoke County to Martinsville. I called it the route of no route because it didn't start from the Wythe County substation and therefore had no route thru Floyd County. It started at Matt Funk and ran straight down to Martinsville. 21 miles shorter than the shortest routing proposed by the power company.

The solicitor told me that if I didn't put this in the testimony package and make it known to the power company it could not be presented in the future even if it was a hundred times better than any route proposed by any and all parties concerned. I wrestled with it knowing there would be consequences. Consequences that a backwoods nobody could come up with a better idea that they had, better than all their high paid engineers and consultants. I just didn't know how right I was.

CHAPTER 9:

MAGIC LAKE

I remember one night during this preparation work, tired and ready to fall asleep, probably around 1 am. I looked out the bedroom sliding door and like magic a lake appeared in front of me. I was a chilly still night with a full moon hanging over the Haycocks. It was very bright and still, not a cloud in the skies. The moon was so bright only a handful of stars could be seen anywhere near the moon and they were probably planets. This lake appeared, as out of nowhere extending from a few hundred feet from the house all the way across the valley to the Blue Ridge Mountains. The bright moonlight was also reflecting off the magical lake making it seem even brighter. It was a heavy fog that settled in quietly that night. I walked out the bedroom door in my slippers as if to reach out and touch it. But the ground was cold and damp and I rethought the better of it as my slippers were soaking wet with ground dew. In all my years living there that was the only night this mystical vision of nature at her best appeared for me. Was this an omen of things to come?

We made about 10 copies of the 100 plus page manuscript of my testimony. The first person to get a complete copy was my boss, Art Guepe. I wasn't going to do anything without his approval. He took it home with him that night and the next morning came in all smiles and congratulated me on this real good work. He loved my new design criteria and said they all made sense and wished me good luck with it. That night in the 1ST week of February I told the group to send it out the next day.

Then the clock started ticking. This is probably the sequence of events from the time we sent it to Appalachian Power Company. Tick, tick, tick; they signed for it at the power companies attorney's office and Appalachian Power Company picked it up from their office. Tick, tick, time passes and the power company reads thru the details of my submittal. Reading thru the first 50 plus pages and then finding my proposed routings taking another 50 pages or so behind. The draftsman would start with route 1 page 1 working the route from starting point to terminal point. When completed then proceed to route 2 plotting them both out with precision. After finishing the 2 routes previously presented at the prior meetings for all to see, along comes a surprise. A 3rd route they haven't heard about. Having done drafting work as part of my job as county engineer and having worked with draftsmen at other positions I held, I had a good idea of the time it would take the engineering staff at the power company to review and plot the new lines having been in charge of drafting and engineering forces previously. I anticipated 10 days to complete the plotting and reviewing of my work. Also, they would have been shocked by the new route of "no route". Let me make this very clear, only 5 people knew about the new routing. Myself, the pilot but he didn't know about the siting, the secretary that types the dictation without seeing where the lines were, the County Solicitor who knew nothing about the siting or start point, just that there was a new line 2 weeks before the submittals and my boss, Art Guepe. Tick, tick, less than two weeks pass and the call comes in for me to go to the County Administrator's office.

CHAPTER 10:

LETS PLAY

Mr. Clark lived in the most prestigious housing developments in Roanoke Valley. You know, the one with the exclusive country club. The one where all the high profile company executives, business owners. lawyers etc. lived. Apparently one of William F. Clark's neighbors was the vice president or president of Appalachian Power Company. Mr. Clark had a good working relationship with Appalachian Power Company as his previous job was City engineer for The City of Roanoke, Virginia. One of his major jobs was purchasing power for all the uses Roanoke City had, buildings, parks, street lighting, etc.. This gave him an opportunity to know and work with the power company officials in the past.

I do not know what happened that night, but I can only imagine what may have happened to spark a sequence of events that was to come.

Sometime during the 3rd week in February his power company neighbor calls Bill inviting him over to his house for a game of cards that he holds along with other industry leaders. You know, the railroad, the steel manufacturing plant and other vice president of the power company.

Greeting Bill with: "We have been noticing the nice work you have been doing with running the county. You know we have a position open on the Country Club Board and we would like for you to consider your name for that slot." Now that is a good way to soften up the pigeon. Bill gets guided to a room with a card table filled with players waiting for him to take the last seat. As the game progresses on, one might think it was a Monopoly game with electric company represented by Appalachian Power Company, the railroad represented by Norfolk and Western Railroad and water works represented by Mr. Clark as the head of Roanoke County and the Municipal Utilities Authority water and sewer facilities.

At 11:00 PM the card game breaks up with all congratulating Mr. Clark on his shoe in nomination to the country club board. Bill is the last one to leave and he is stopped by Appalachian Power Company president. He and wants to know what an engineer in Roanoke County employment under him is doing designing power lines. "Did you, Bill, as the County Administrator sanction this work? This has a major effect on our company plans and is costing us time and money. Would you allow one of your employees to work on company time to harass us? See what you can do, I would be greatly appreciative if you did."

CHAPTER 11:

THE NEXT MORNING

Walking into the Public Works Department on the 2nd floor where my office was, the secretary points up to the ceiling and tells me to go upstairs. Mr. Clark wants to see me directly without going thru my boss, Art. He expresses a stern and clear concern for a county employee getting involved with outside activities. Especially high profile cases where Roanoke County may be involved. He continues going on and on about me not getting involved with the power company and its plans. That I would be risking my position if I were to testify before the State Corporation Commission in March. He states how I'm just a county employee and then the words began to blur as my head was hurting more and more as his animosity towards me got stronger and stronger. I explained all this was done on my own private time, weekends mostly and many nights. I strongly affirmed that at no time did I indicate to anyone that I was representing Roanoke County in anyway other than this was just my place of employment. I answered all his accusations with a simple "Art has been in the loop all the time and he approved of this." He made a simple call downstairs and got Art to bring up his copy of my testimony. Art nodded as he answered and said he was very aware and approved of this. I got out of this pickle jar, but I knew I hit a nerve, a very big one.

I had expected some kickback from Appalachian Power Company. This came precisely at the time when it did as it following the timetable I had set in my mind for the power company engineering staff to complete go over my testimony. Upon review, the engineering staff should have kicked it up to upper level management. Then upon the higher ups review, call their attorney's and have them handle it back through the channel it came from. I totally anticipated the call to come from the Floyd County solicitor. This is the way it should have come back if they were playing fair.

They were playing dirty and made it personal. They had no business putting ideas into Mr. Clark's head about my private life. This hurt me where it hurts the most. My job, my family and my dignity. I didn't tell Ginny about this as she didn't need to know about the additional pressure placed upon us. Oh yes, another burden as she was carrying our 3rd child. They made this effect my family and my way of life. How did I know this, intuition maybe, but I got a sense within me that picks these things up.

CHAPTER 12:

LOST AT SEA

When I turned 12, one of the strangest events happened to me, ever, ever. The local Kawanis business club sends a needing child to summer camp every summer and that year I was chosen as being the neediest child in Hicksville, Long Island, NY. I got to go to camp that summer which was located along the north shore of Long Island, probably 50 miles or more from my home. The camp was located on a high bluff overlooked the waters of the Long Island Sound and was heavily wooded to the south of the campsite with no homes nearby. It was fun; we always had something to do. All these kids and nobody cared about where you came from. Archery, hand crafts, swimming and canoeing were many of my favorites. To go swimming in the Long Island Sound we had to traverse down the cliff with over 100 steps, but nobody was counting. But, I do remember counting them once. I always had a thing with numbers. It was late in July, the camp was very quiet at night except for the occasional snore from one of 12 boys in each screened in hut with 6 bunk beds. I had a bottom bunk. There was one light in the middle of the hut and that was off. We were about 100 feet from the main meetinghouse and dining hall. We had no TV's and no radios at the camp. You didn't need any.

Then there was this one night I awoke at around 1:00 AM or later on the morning of July 26, 1956 hearing strange noises, yelling and screaming. I felt pressure coming from everywhere. I jumped out of bed and all was quiet. The lights were out, everyone was sleeping and there was only an occasional snore. I laid back down and the voices and the turmoil returned. I felt deeply disturbed and got up again. Nothing, absolute quiet, only a slight mist in a somewhat cool summer night. I walked around a bit, all the way to the meetinghouse and dining hall and still nothing. Again, returning to my bed, I lay down and again the turmoil returned. I put my hands over my ears, my eyes tightly shut, but that didn't help the noise. I couldn't get to sleep. This continued for most of the night until I finally succumb to sleep from exhaustion. Funny, nobody else woke up; nobody else heard noises, just me.

Morning finally arrived and I was in a stupor of tiredness. Maybe I got 2 hours of sleep. Looking around, everybody was doing the same morning routines since we got there. Breakfast as normal, games and activities began. It was our cabin's day to get into the war canoe, a big 20+ person canoe. Paddling out into the sound, we all noticed a submarine sitting on the surface a few hundred yards away. We all came to the conclusion at the same time to chase it and maybe catch up to it and board it like pirates. We must have scared it away as we closed in as it sped away, dove and then disappeared under the water. It was the only day during our 2-week stay at summer camp that we saw a submarine. Another oddity, all day long Navy planes were flying low over our camp area and I would waive to the pilots as they flew by. Thinking nothing of again, I finished the final week at camp. I didn't mention this to anybody at camp as I was not sure what had happened.

At the end of the week in early August I finally got home, my mother picked me up from the bus drop off spot. When we got home she sat me down and in an unusual voice told me that something bad had happened while I was away. In the early dense foggy morning of July 26, 1956 the Swedish freighter Stockholm had a fateful meeting with the pride of Italy, the Andrea Doria, crashing broadsided into the luxury liner. After about 10 hours of slowly sinking it finally went to the bottom off the coast of Long Island in the Atlantic Ocean. Over 50 people lost their lives that night....and I was there. I can distinctly remember a hallway with people pushing their way thru, but that is all I remembered of the incident. We had known a family that was on the ocean liner that fateful day. Was there a connection, I do not know.

CHAPTER 13:

THE TOWN MEETING

To further complicate matters, my wife, Virginia was 3 months pregnant with our third, a girl to be born in September. It was difficult enough on a public employee's salary to get by. I certainly couldn't make it on unemployment insurance. A week before the hearing I was walking up the stairway to my 2nd floor office when Mr. Clark was coming down from the 3rd floor. It was faster than the elevators. When he saw me as he made the U-turn in between floors, he started to huff up and his face turned red. My skull felt like it was going to explode and feelings of hate projected into me. Luckily he just passed me by without saying a word. It felt like a massive tornado was coming at you but just missed. But somehow the meaning was loud and clear.

The night before the State Corporation Commission hearing I called the solicitor and told him about the pressure being put on me, that Mr. Clark actually told me not to testify, that it could cost me my job. He told me I had only 2 options. Number one, obviously, was not to testify and my submitted testimony would not be read into the record. All the work on the project would be lost and I would have let down the Citizens for the Preservation of Floyd County. Plus, I would have been untrue to myself, my moral fiber was screaming that

I needed to testify. He also told me that I needed to tell the State Corporation Commission about this incident by reading a prepared statement into the proceedings. I needed to tell them that I was being pressured by my employer who had ties with highly positioned members of Appalachian Power Company not to testify.

That night when I was called to the witness stand I was sworn in giving my name and occupation. I acknowledged my written testimony as mine and it was so duly entered into the proceedings without further testimony. I asked if I could read something to the commissioners and become part of the record. It was agreed to. I started out with something like: My father gave his life for this country, for our freedoms so that I may have the right to participate in hearings like this. But pressure is being put on me by my employer not to testify and abandon these proceedings and withdraw my testimony...... Let me tell you that the meeting at the Floyd County Courthouse was packed to overflowing. Many in attendance were attorneys for the power company and ranking officials from the power company. I knew I did it. I stepped into a boiling pot of water with no shoes on. Ginny stayed home with the kids as she wasn't involved with the Citizens For the Preservation of Floyd County, she had only gone out with the group during the florescent light bulbs excursion under the 765 Kva line and that was the extent of her involvement.

That night I lay awake in bed thinking about that evening's hearings and worrying about my family, my job and my security. I knew phones were ringing in Roanoke. Early that night as I lay in bed, I couldn't sleep. I could feel my heart pounding in my chest and it wouldn't stop pounding. Then I felt a welling up in my chest. The pressure built up inside my chest area and I realized that my heart wasn't beating. Seconds went by like minutes and I knew I had to do something. I scrunched my shoulders together and hardened my stomach while jerking myself into a ball position. Nothing, I did it again even harder and then, thump, a huge rushing feeling went thru my chest, a very large heartbeat rang throughout my body and the next and the next until it reached normal. How much more stress could I take? Morning would come soon enough.

This time I did make the news by my own actions, big news. That next morning I walked into the office and was immediately directed into the County Administrators office. I walked into Mr. Clarks office and sat down. Mr. William F. Clark had eyes of steel penetrating into me. His face turned red and redder by the minute. Next to him stood the County Attorney, Mr. Ed Natt with his law degree from The University of Richmond in Virginia. He was about 6 foot 5 inches tall and very slim and usually didn't say much when I was around except when the gang of employees went to lunch at the local Hardee's burger joint. He would always be talking about basketball, one of my least favorite sports. He stood directly to the right side of Mr. Clark as Mr. Clark sat behind his desk and slightly behind Mr. Clark.

After what seemed like a long time of silence, the first words out of Mr. Clark's mouth were "YOU'RE FIRED" and he went on while the Ed Natt, the County Attorney started to squeeze his right shoulder with his left hand. I could hear him softly saying; "You can't fire him" over and over into his ear until Mr. Clark calmed down. This would be a violation of my civil rights. I felt like a little dog being kicked over and over. This couldn't be happening to me. My life is over. Then Mr. Clark conferred with the attorney quietly. I could only hear a few words. He then turned to me and said I could keep my job only if I rescinded my testimony and I asked the Virginia State Corporation Commission to withdraw all of it from the record.

He gave me two weeks to do it. I was reeling from this meeting when I left. I could hardly walk and I could not focus. But as the day went on it became perfectly clear why he was doing this, why the only the thing I had to do was remove all my testimony presented before the commission. He has no real knowledge as to my testimony and didn't care. Someone else was pulling his string.... Hard.

Needless to say the two weeks passed and I didn't pull my testimony. But, I never heard about this from Mr. Clark again. Not the least to say he still emanated hate towards me. Once again I didn't tell Ginny as not to worry her especially while she was pregnant.

Yes. I knew I was put in my place and that was the last of my involvement with the Citizens for the Preservation of Floyd County. The State Corporation Commissioners would hold meetings in other impacted communities, but I was no longer involved. I couldn't get involved with it anymore. I did what I was asked to do for the citizens group and got my testimony into the record. True this almost cost me my job. But, all was not forgiven. As the years passed an uneasy truce between Mr. William F. Clark and myself existed. I just kept my mouth shut and did my job. And I did it well.

One of my duties was keeping the tax maps correct seemed to be a never-ending job, as previous administrations had not maintained the maps well. A sixty-year-old man came to me with a deed for a 1,500 acre tract. He wanted to know how much land he really had. We looked into the records and could find nothing in Roanoke County. I told him I would look into it. I followed the deed back to the division of a 40,000 acre land grant that was surveyed by Thomas Jefferson in 1795. As it turned out it was more like 60,000 acres.

There were at least 10 parcels in the original survey of over 1,000 acres each or much more. At the time of the survey there was only 1 county the property was in, adjacent Montgomery County.   In 1838 Roanoke County was cut off from Montgomery County and 2/3 of the original land surveyed remained in Montgomery county. Unfortunately this man's land was in Roanoke County, but he had been paying taxes in Montgomery County. This took quite some time. I was finding parcels of land that were plotted on other tax maps 2 to 3 or more miles from their real locations. Every deed from existing tax parcels had to be found before it could be plotted, if it could be found. The translations and adjustments had to be made from deed to deed, from era to era and things constantly changed. The old charter oaks were gone where the surveys began. Old records were in rods and poles, chains and links, tree-to-tree and following a stream down to a point. Then survey descriptions changed to "adjacent to lands of" an adjacent landowner and then to modern day surveys with distances and directions and set survey points. I was able to identify about 900 acres of land that was owned by others, mostly with squatter's rights of openly owing the land and declaring ownership and paying taxes for 20 years or from tax sales where the county tax collector was actually able to identify a piece that had not been paying taxes.

On his final visit, I handed him a copy of the new revised tax map, told him I was 90% certain about the land left, but all that was left was steep mountainside and gullies. This land had been in his family for generations and the owners were paying taxes on it since 1795 but not in Roanoke County.

CHAPTER 14:

BAD BOYS

I was given a handful of tickets to a Virginia Tech football game. On my salary that was a treat. I didn't miss a game while I was at Virginia Tech. I even went to a couple of disappointing bowl games. The drive to the stadium from Floyd was about 25 miles. In order to get to Virginia Tech most roads went thru Christiansburg. The back road into Radford and the road into West Virginia were excepted. During the days at college, we liked to explain to people how to get to Blacksburg. It wasn't nice so I won't repeat it.

Driving to the game about halfway between Christiansburg and Blacksburg there is a long downward sloping hill with a few billboards along the east side of the northbound lane. As I drove by it I noticed that the coke bottle shaped hole about 5 feet in from the leading edge was still there and that brought back memories of my stay there. Only Joe and I knew how that hole got there, at about 115 miles per hour.

I was from the north and was going to a southern military college with over local 90% southern boys in the freshman class. It didn't take me long to know that they were 2 to 4 years behind in the street skills of us northern boys. Case in point: On Thanksgiving Day the entire Virginia Tech Corps marched thru Roanoke as did the Virginia Military Institute Corps in a once yearly football rivalry. After the game all the freshmen, myself included, swamped the town. My drinking days were over in high school. I made a promise to myself that I would not get drunk again while attending college. But, that day, the other freshmen in my squadron were doing beer chugs in a local bar near the stadium. They saw me walk by and began to cat call me because I wouldn't join them chugging beers. I told them to leave me alone, I didn't drink. But they continued making jokes about the Yankee sissy. I told them if they really wanted me to, set one up. 5 or more classmates were in a line holding their beer glasses waiting for the call. GO. Up, gulp, down, bam. What, done in 2 seconds and most of the others weren't halfway thru. I just walked away and they never bothered me again. The rat year was really hell, again as a Yankee in a southern populated school I was picked out on a regular basis to visit upperclassmen's rooms where I would have to stand at attention with rifle at Port Arms, with a 3 x 5 card under my chin and a pencil between my shoulder blade for an hour reciting school required data and facts. If you made it thru an hour, they usually let me go, usually. But there were times the stay lasted more than 2 hours. Yankee rats were different from southern rats, and maybe they were trying to get me to quit.

When walking thru the halls, freshman were required to hug the corridor wall, should an upperclassman be standing there a salutation of "Good Evening Mr.", name inserted, "Sir" was required. One day as I was whizzing thru the halls I passes an open door and gave the proper salutation. "Halt Rat" came ringing from the room now behind me. How did you know it was me, that isn't my room? "Just did, Sir, don't know why, just did Sir." It was uncanny the way I was able to sense someone's presence and know how exactly who it was. I guess it was a defense my mind developed to keep me from having to spend an uneventful evening in an upperclassman's room with rifle in hand.

Joe and I were two northern boys who constantly broke the rules when we got to be upperclassmen. When our ready cash got low, we would sneak out after taps going into town to play pool for money. The pool hall was located behind the bus stop and restaurant opposite the main entrance to campus and the quad where our barracks were. Here we played eight ball, but mostly nine ball and we usually won playing 50 cents on a money balls and $1 on the nine ball. We both left with more money than we came with. We usually closed the place down at 2 am, sneaking back in I would finish my homework, dive into the bottom rack and sleep for 3 hours until 1st call for Growley (breakfast). Luckily, I chose not to have a roommate as there were plenty of open rooms those years as 50% of the rat class washed out, one of the highest washout rates in the schools history. My top bunk was made up as prescribed with bedding so tight you could bounce a quarter a couple of inches into the air. I slept in the bottom bunk with no bedding and no mess to make up.

CHAPTER 15:

FATE STRIKES

Driving back and forth to Blacksburg and Long Island I would drive thru the Shenandoah Valley. During the moonlight nights, goose bumps would propagate throughout my entire body, hairs standing at attention. I could feel the presence of the Confederate Army under General Stonewall Jackson marching thru the back woods and the mountain passes. I my mind I could hear the clanging of mess kits and canteens as they skirted around the Northern Union Army to another skirmish site. I wasn't a one-time thing. These feelings ran thru me only at night, only during moonlit nights, and only in the Shenandoah Valley. What was the connection that made these feelings run though my body?

One incident that most influenced my future was the squadron graduation party from military college when freshmen became upperclassmen and seniors left. Our unit's party in June of 1966 was on a farm outside campus in rural Blacksburg, Virginia. My mother had purchased a new 396 Chevelle for me and I brought it down for graduation. I only had a few beers that day as I really didn't like draft beer much at all. One cadet ex-rat was really wasted and I decided to take him back to the barracks. The road was curvy and in a depression with both sides elevated above the car. As I navigated my way back to campus I downshifted the vehicle by depressing the clutch and stepping on the gas and put the car into lower gear, a standard process that I was very good at. But, the vehicle sped up and I took my foot off the gas. It went out of control running up the embankment and crashing into and under a fence until it stopped in a field. Nobody was hurt, just a fencepost. But, I got a reckless driving ticket for my efforts. Found guilty I paid my fine and went on my merry way. But, the Air Force found out about this in their final evaluation and cancelled my flight schools in Texas for fighter jet training. I was washed out totally for this incident. Two months later, General Motors came out with a report that the vehicle never had motor mounts in it from the factory and they offered a cash settlement. The gas pedal linkage collapsed as the motor rocked back not being secured onto the frame and that rocking motion depressed the gas pump on the carburetor making the high power vehicle speed up out of control and crash. But, too late to help my desire to fly. That year and the ones to follow the U.S. Air Force lost more fighter pilots as they decided to bomb North Vietnam. I look at it this way, I probably would have been one of those downed pilots and this twist of fate kept me from loosing my life once again.

In another turn, I ended up in the army and with my special skills as a Civil Engineer. I was sent to Yuma Proving Grounds. During the Vietnam War many of our troops were killed by our own artillery from "short rounds" that didn't have enough power when shot to get over the front lines and landed on our own positions. As a result of that, a small percent of all mortar and artillery rounds were required to be tested. Hundreds of freight cars waited in the Yuma, Arizona rail sidings for random samples to be taken and tested for compliance on its way to San Diego for loading into cargo ships going to Vietnam.

Contrary to movie lovers everywhere, small 88 mm mortars do not blow up towers in a massive fireball. They spread out shrapnel, rocks and debris pelting all around. How do I know? You guessed it, I was in one of those towers day after day watching mortar rounds come in, 88's and 4.2's. I recorded their azimuth of the impact from the tower. The data collected was plotted for each round fired. That was used to calculate the landing spot of the round with a minimum of two intersecting lines from reporting towers, but 3 towers were always used. Twice the mortars tried to get me, once an 88 mm mortar shell landed 20 feet from the tower and another time one landed right between the front legs pelting the under decking with shrapnel. That was close, real close.

That was nothing like what was to come. The Army was doing lots of experimental testing at this location, like the day they flew a B-25 bomber over at low altitude. They had an experimental cluster bomb attached to it. This ordinance is now widely used as an anti-personnel bomb. We sat in articulating domes and took high-speed photography of the plane flying by. We cough the moment of the disbursement of the clusters as they were dropped from the plane. The next day we had to locate each by survey and map out the location of every one of these 1,500 special shaped bomblet and all were labeled according to their location within the bombshell. What a fun job that was, walking the desert in the midst of scorpions, rattlesnakes and black widow spiders. But you got used to the 120+ daily temperatures. Each man got a 5 gallon jug of drinking water every day going out and I never once brought a jug back with water therein. Drinking water all day long and sweating in the hot sun without an ounce of wetness.

In another mind busting experiment, the army wanted to extended the projected distance of its 155 mm Long Tom mobile cannon artillery shells by putting in a rocket timed fused booster designed to go off 2.5 seconds after firing. One of my first jobs with this project was to stand directly behind the cannon and time the shell, watching it fly downrange looking for the fuse to ignite. Then hit the stopwatch when the fuse ignited the booster and record the time from firing the cannon. The other job was to make sure the cannon was properly aligned after every shot. The next week we rotated. I went down range while the down range team went behind the gun. I was set up over a survey point in the middle of nowhere 20+ miles downrange from the gun. Watching these big shells come in from a distance was something frightful. These were aimed to hit about ½ mile away from my survey point. You can hear them coming in and actually see them as they landed. The thud was loud even at that distance and the explosions massive, tearing up trees and foliage. My job was to sight in on the explosion and record the angle to it. These shells were also shaped on the inside designed to break apart and become long narrow lawnmower like blades spinning around chopping everything or anybody to pieces within 50 meters from point if impact.

One day, just like every other day, hot and cloudless. It was past midday when the sound of an incoming round was so much stronger than usual. I looked up into the sky almost whitened by the high midday sun and saw this black object coming directly towards me. There was nowhere to hide, just barren ground. I stood there and watched it come in and hit the ground no more than 30 feet from me. I didn't flinch. I didn't crap in my pants, but, I watched it bounce out of the ground about 8 feet into the air then snake across the ground directly in front of me, then come to rest about 40 feet beyond me.... A dud. That was the only dud in all my time spent with the 155 mm project. Minutes later a jeep appeared racing out to my position knowing the shell had come down near me and I just pointed to it, I never said another word about it until now. That closed down the range for that day.

Later that week while stationed on the point, sometime early in the day the pick-up vehicle came out with the others and drove back us back to the barracks. Later, back at the barracks, I found out that the entire gun crew of six working on the Long Tom was killed when a shell being loaded into the breach exploded, thus ending the project. Shortly thereafter ending my stay at Yuma Proving Grounds. I guess I was lucky again as we were slated to rotate behind the gun the very next week. Either one of those incidents could have ended my life. I sometimes still imagine I didn't have a dud land on my position. In my own worst nightmare I imagine that it killed me, blasting my body into mist. Only my boots were found. I dream that I'm living another life somewhere in an alternate universe. Or was it a divine hand of providence protecting me for some later encounter with my life?

While at Yuma Proving Grounds, one of my classmates came to be stationed at Yuma proving grounds. He was from "F" Troop and I was from "C" Squadron. We spent some time together and became great friends even though we didn't really know each other while at Virginia Tech. Shortly after the accident, orders were handed out to most of the base after the deadly accident with the 155 mm cannon. Most of the active personnel were transferred out. I went east to Germany and he went west to Vietnam. His wife became great friends with my college sweetheart, who I married the June after I got out of the service, as they were both seniors at Radford College. I never heard from him again as on his last day in Vietnam on the bus to the airport for the flight home, a grenade was thrown into the bus where he was sitting and he was killed. I remember seeing his name etched in the War Memorial Chapel at the end of the entrance boulevard onto the campus. His name was the only name from the class of '66 that

I saw from over 1,100 graduates that year at the time that I visited it. I moved my fingers over the letters as if to say goodbye to a good friend.

While in Germany, I was stationed in Heidelberg with the 656 Engineers, speaking a little German I quickly became the company interpreter. Our operations in the middle of the cold war brought us into the field along the Czechoslovakian border doing highly classified 1st order survey work for launch sites for the mobile Long John nuclear tipped rocket launchers. Going into anymore detail would be a breach of my top secret clearance. We would go into these small villages where I would arrange a week stay at a time with food and lodging for our small company. Of course I did the survey work too. One German town, which we seemed to like better than others was Amorbach, located in the heart of the Odenwald Forest.

CHAPTER 16:

A SOLDIER'S LIFE

One day the company commander grabbed me and requested (ordered) that I accompany him into the northern sector where some damage claims were made about a previous NATO maneuver there. One of the most interesting experiences occurred to me during this trip. We were passing thru a quaint and very old town somewhere south of Essen. We decided to stop here for lunch. There was this picture perfect old Gasthaus in the middle of town and it was the only restaurant in town from where we were. A relatively large single room dining hall with wooden support beams and a 2 story high ceiling. Just like those in mid-evil era movies. When we walked in, the place was virtually empty except for a little old man sitting in the far corner. All along the outer walls were old pictures of military men beginning from my left circling to the other walls. I went from table to table, wall to wall and at the very end was the old man slouched over sipping a bowl of soup.

It began with old time pictures of the Prussian Era military. I couldn't stop gazing, then later a young teen in a brown shirt uniform, the German equivalent of a militaristic boy scout, then to someone in a storm troopers uniform. Eventually an older man in a colonel's uniform.

Out from the kitchen came this stocky man in his 50's. He saw me looking at the pictures and I recognized him as the younger man in the early pictures. Pointing at the pictures, I asked him in German about the pictures. I made a guess that the old man sitting in the corner was the man on the horse. He told me to sit and began to tell me a story I'll never forget.

Yes, I was correct, that was his father in the corner. He has served under Von Hindenburg in the late 1800's and was a part of an elite brigade of soldiers that marched from country to country throughout Europe showing off their military grandeur as a way of keeping other countries aware of the German military might. This was a force of horse mounted calvary and marching foot soldier brigade that didn't go out for war, but to keep the peace. They would go out on maneuvers for a year or more at time. Eventually, as time progressed the old man in the corner was promoted to colonel. There was this one picture of him proudly mounted on a white horse. Next to him were mechanized armored cars, the old regime meeting the new regime. But, he was old school and just after Germany invaded Poland he was forced to retire in favor of the new regime.

Meanwhile, the youth was one of the first to enlist in the brown shirts somewhere In the early 1930's. He later became a part of an elite German storm trooper unit. Eventually he was sent into Stalingrad. He said he went home for a 2 week leave around Christmas time and that was the last time he saw his wife and parents. Sometime shortly after returning to the front, the German army in Stalingrad surrendered to the Russian forces where he became one of 250,000 German prisoners. This began with the historic forced to march all the way into Siberia. He stated less than 50,000 German soldiers made it there alive. His wife, who then became pregnant with their first child during his time on leave, never heard from him after that last visit home before returning to Stalingrad. Everyone thought the worst. No news of him after the war ended. All thought he had died as so many had during the battle for Stalingrad and during the thousand-mile forced march into Siberia. The war ended in 1945, but the Russians refused to let anyone know there were still prisoners alive in Siberia. That was when the family gave up. The Russians said they had no prisoners left at the end of the war. When he was finally released in 1952, less than 5,000 remained of the 250,000 original prisoners. He arrived home to the joyful surprise of his wife and parents. He got to meet his 10-year-old daughter, whom he didn't even know about. They were still there running the family business with his father. He asked me about my father. I flat out told him that my father was killed in WWII and that I never got to see him, but he died in the Pacific fighting the Japanese, not the Germans. His wife came out and brought us our lunch. What a difference a few dozen pictures make. One thing I do remember, with all the Germans that I met during my stay in Germany, anyone that had fought in World War II, none, not a one had ever fought against the Americans. I guess they said that as they were embarrassment to admit that they had fought against the Americans as we were now their friends and allies.

I was starting my 2nd winter in Germany when orders came in. The entire 656 Engineers was being shipped out to Vietnam on Thanksgiving Day. That morning as we were packing up our duffle bags and heading for transportation a representative from the Red Cross came into the barracks and asked to see me. He handed me an envelope and said you're going home on the next available flight on an emergency leave. My mother was dying with late stage cancer and requested I be brought home as a sole surviving son. That very day my unit went east to Vietnam and this time I went west. Another twist in fate looking over me, if that was what it was. Once again taken from harm's way.

One thing you really need to know is that when I went home for my first leave in the Army, my mother already had cancer, but she didn't tell me about it. She had prepared me a meal I'll never forget either. She went all out a filled the table with so much food my entire platoon couldn't eat it all. And while I was eating, my mother said "I love you" for the first time ever in all my memories.

CHAPTER 17:

FHA

Farming is difficult, especially when doing it by yourself. It's better to help others and get help in return when you really need it. We had made friends with a couple from Floyd that owned a 188 acre farm about 3 miles from us. They didn't have any children, but they soon would have a heard of milking cows, about 50 if I remember properly. They lived in an old farmhouse that had no heat, just a large fireplace in the middle of the living room. That property had belonged to one of their relatives in the past and they got a FHA loan to buy the farm outright and the herd of cows together with equipment and milking station. All the equipment was used before except for the milking machine. When the cows got there, they were easy to handle, but they had no milk. They got a Bull from a neighbor. Bulls are only needed once a year for a couple of months to make sure all the cows are pregnant, then it is preferable to lend them out for stud and let the other farmer keep and feed him while the bull does his job and impregnates all the cows.

Now it was spring, and the first born calf was named FHA. We were invited over to participate in the celebration. We all went out to see the new calf and mother. The calf was spry and jumping all over.

Ginny went over to pet FHA, but when she got there FHA began to kick and got a hoof Ginny right in the stomach. At this time she was about 6 months pregnant. I rushed her to the hospital as we were both very nervous about this not wanting anything bad to happen to our unborn daughter. I rushed her into the Christiansburg Hospital emergency ward where she had a thorough examination. The baby was fine and was well protected from harm in the mother's womb.

As the summer progressed and all the cows had calved, the job of managing the cows became almost too much to handle. It seemed we would be over there every evening helping with the night milking. I usually ended up on the small bobcat loader pushing manure out of the holding pen and milking area into a big pile to be loaded onto a manure spreader. Then, it would be spread onto the fields as fertilizer. Milking time is when the cows are ready, usually at dawn and dusk as cows don't know how to tell time, and you can't miss a milking or the quantity of milk will decrease. As a repayment for our help, they helped with our plowing and planting, harvesting and silage storage. I could not do it myself as we didn't have the equipment. We didn't keep track of the hours, that didn't matter if we were there more, we got the help we needed when we needed it.

CHAPTER 18:

THE WINTER OF '77

I was running between 15 and 20 head of Black Angus cattle on the farm. My wife stated that I could have any color cow I wanted, but no black and white cows were allowed, as they were milk cows. So I chose all black. These were Angus cows and easy to keep being fairly docile creatures. I had strung electric fencing around most of the farm's perimeter. The most difficult spot was at the upper end of the stream that ran right thru the middle of the farm. At this end there was a steep ravine about 6 feet deep and the trick was to get it blockaded with old split rail fencing and tack some electric fencing on it. Did you know that the grass is always greener on the other side of the fence? At least that's what the cows thought. If they saw a fence in front of them, they always had one of the heard being pushed into it to see if the electricity was working. It is just so comical to see the herd push one of the cows towards the fence as if they drew straws. The chosen would come up inch-by-inch maneuvering its head in a circular motion as if to just miss the electric fence until it got close enough and ZAP. A spark to the wet nose would back that cow off the fence 10 or more feet in an instant. The problem with that spot in the ravine is that during periods of high wind and heavy rain, branches and twigs from the farm above would wash down, get tangled in the fencing and ground out the electric fence. Those were the times I would have to be on fence patrol.

If and when that happened while I was at work, trouble was certainly near. There is an unwritten rule, if a cow can get its head under a fence, the body will always follow, and if one gets out, they will all get out. Around 4 pm one rainy day I get a frantic call from Ginny, the cows were out. I got permission to wrap up early and ran home to help chase some cows. Cows love corn, it is like triple chocolate marshmallow ice cream with whipped cream and cherries on top all in a bucket to them. A neighbor had called and said those cows were trotting down the back road about a mile from the farm. Ginny knew just what to do. She grabbed a bucket and filled it with corn, drove past the cows and came back with the bucket in her hand and hanging out the window. The cow followed her all the way back to the farm. Needless to say I spent half that evening cleaning out the ravine and getting the fence working again.

January is the usually coldest month of the year. This year it was colder, much colder. The end of the 3rd week in January the jet stream settled over Floyd County. A large thermometer was placed just outside our kitchen window and was quite accurate. It went from +120 degrees to −20 degrees. One day around January 20th the temperature went below −20 degrees and the next day the mercury didn't even come out of the bulb. The wind sounded like a freight train running right thru our living room for days without end. When the noise from the wind died down, it was still blowing at 20 miles per hour. I didn't have a way to measure the speed of the wind, but it must have been close to hurricane velocity. This continued on for over a week until one morning the wind stopped and the temperature dropped. The sun poked its nose over the mountains indicating it was time to feed the cows. The moisture that came out of my mouth made a long stream before it dissipated in the distance. It was really cold. I had a corn silage pit dug into the side of the top of the hill near the cornfield and close to the house, less than one hundred feet from the corner of the house.

The top of the silage pit was covered with black plastic and about one hundred old tires to help keep the plastic down. That previous summer we entered our crop in the county fair and came in 2nd place for yield. It might have been 1st place, but I'm not bragging. The silage corn fermented into a pickled stew under that black plastic. That drove the cows wild, especially when there wasn't anything else to eat. It's like legal moonshine for cows. The pickling process actually produced heat and kept the silage from freezing, usually. Every morning at the break of dawn I had to feed the cows. MOOOOO COOOOW would ring out of my mouth from my hilltop where I stood to the valley below. The cows could hear that call from wherever they were hiding to keep out from the cold. They came in a hurry and knew just where to line up in the feeding area close to the electric fence. The colder it was the more I had to feed them. This morning as in the past few frigid mornings I had to bring a sledge hammer with me to break out the frozen barrier of silage on the front face to get to the not yet frozen silage and bust up the frozen clumps to a feeding size. As I pulled the plastic back, I was startled by a small bird fluttering out from a warm spot inside the silage pit behind the black plastic flap. That was unusual to say the least. I began to hammer the front face of the silage that was frozen about 1 foot thick. Then another animal scooted out. A feral cat had gone in after the bird and lost it in the night. The cat went speeding out about 20 yards, stopped, changed direction and ran some more only to stop again on go off into a different direction. This very disorientated cat did this over and over again until it disappeared into the underbrush. I figured the cat was only hours from freezing to death and had no idea where it was. The cows lined up along the electric fence feeding area and they were looking at that cat too. It took a long time that day to finish feeding the cows. When I got back in and took off my gloves, my knuckles were frost bitten. I ran cold well water over my hands for about 15 minutes until the feeling came back. It wasn't a good feeling either; sharp, stinging and penetrating. Even today when it's cold my knuckles get discolored in a weird reddish sheen and remind me. One good thing, the electric was still on. Oh, did I just speak too soon?

That night the snows came and the wind picked up again, this time over a foot of snow knocking out all the main power lines into Floyd County. Our electric heaters didn't work, the well didn't work and there were no lights and no electric going to the stove to cook on. We had backup plans plus, we didn't have to worry about the refrigerator or the freezer being off. Plus, the electric bill will be really low for the month. Total electric living does have its built in drawbacks. Luckily I had 3 wood burning stoves, one for the bedroom area, one for the living area and the smaller pot belly stove in the kitchen, and we got by. We got our drinking and cooking water from melting big pots filled with snow. You had to make sure it was fresh white snow. Not walked on or yellow snow. Cooking on top of the wood stoves and seeing by candlelight everywhere. We couldn't take baths, but washed ourselves down with washcloths by the wood stoves. One would think with the electric out, the cows would be running thru the streets of downtown Floyd. But, they stayed in a thicket of woods huddled together and didn't go out into the cold except to eat. Now, with a couple of feet of snow on the ground one might think the cows couldn't be fed, but we did and they loved it. I threw the corn silage on top of the snow-covered ground and they ate it all including the snow down to the ground. We eat snow cones don't we?

Around February 4th we had a celebration, the electric was back on and the temperature rose bringing the mercury out of the bulb and it hit −16 degrees around noon. Winter released its grip and the schools were back in session. I had been going into work every day. The roads were safe since there was only one stoplight in the County of Floyd at the intersection of the 2 main roads running thru the county, Floyd being at the crossroads in the center of town.

CHAPTER 19:

3S3

Time always passes quicker than we can understand and things happen for a reason. Less than a year afterwards the hearings held in Floyd I heard from a different group of citizens wanting the help of an expert witness. Someone that was accepted by the State Corporation Commission and considered an expert on matters at hand. In reality, someone that wasn't afraid to testify against the power company. Somehow, I became a celebrity in the this field as the State Corporation Commission recognized me as an expert witness. They wanted me to review plans by Appalachian Power Company to build a new pump storage facility in the wilderness of the mountains and state forest lands in Virginia. A pump storage facility is where 2 large lakes are on either side of a hydroelectric generation station located inside the dam. During the day when demand for electricity is high, the water Is routed thru the generators producing electricity while the water fills up the lower lake. At night when the power consumption is low, excess power from Appalachian Power's coal fired generating plants that can't be turned off just for a few hours at night diverts the excess electricity to the dam and pump the water from the lower dam up to the upper dam for reuse the next day. This is a very highly efficient process.

I agreed to look into it. I expected to get something to read about the case, but there wasn't any time for that. They said that they just needed the name of their expert witness to be submitted tomorrow for the hearing is in a couple of days. What did I get myself into again?

When I finally got to Abingdon, Virginia. This is way down in the southwest corner of Virginia nestled in between West Virginia, Kentucky and Tennessee. This is where the Virginia State Corporation Commission was holding its hearing. Then I briefly met him. A fairly tall man of slight build maybe an inch or two bigger than my six foot frame. And he was carrying a Bible with him to the hearings. He introduced himself as S. Strother Smith III. He greeted me and asked that I stand outside until formalities had concluded and not to come in until they needed me, if they needed me. My name was accepted as their witness but the power company pulled its request for a license at this time. I would like to think that my name had something to do with their withdrawing their application but I got off easy. Mr. Smith liked my candor and willingness to help those who could not help themselves, he asked me if he could use me in the future, and like a fool I agreed. HERE WE GO AGAIN

Later in the year of 1977 I got a call from Strother Smith. I said he could call me anytime, but I didn't think it would be this soon. He was letting me know that Appalachian Power Company had filed for a $165 million rate increase with the State Corporation Commission. This rate increase would raise the average customer's bill by about $10.00 a month.

As it turned out this was tied into my previous power line construction fight. This rate increase was for the funding and construction of these lines and power plants and projected growth needs well into the future. Plus for what the company called A.F.U.D.C.. I had never heard of it. He said somewhat hesitantly "Allowance for Funds Used During Construction". I didn't know what that was and neither did he. Strother asked me what information we should request from Appalachian Power Company.

Not knowing what information I needed for this, I shot for the moon. If I didn't ask for it, I wouldn't get it. I said I wanted it all, all the past power generation records and construction projects for the past 20 years and for the projected growth for next 20 years into the future just to be a stickler. I never in my wildest dreams thought I was going to get anything worthwhile.

Well, you know what overloading the system does to someone just like an old time computer. They tried to do the crash and burn trick to me. American Electric Power, the parent company for Appalachian Power company sent me boxes and boxes of records from all of its 7 operation arms including Appalachian Power Company. These were delivered to my house and dropped off in the driveway.

I emptied them onto the kitchen table which was an extra-long wood table. I stacked them into piles. One pile for each of the separate operating arms which were then broken down into different modes and sources in a spread sheet layout monthly for each of the 20 years of past service I requested. After that there was the proposed construction of new generation plants and their supporting power lines, their location, capacity and projected costs. This information was broken down by the order of when they were projected to be built. And then there was this final piece of the puzzle that broke down source of outside power purchased and sold by American Electric Power company. When I got finished the table was completely full of piles of light blue covered booklets about one foot tall each stack. I started thumbing thru the piles to get a grip on just what they sent me. I began to realize that what I was given was the Rosetta Stone I needed encrusted with jewels.

Jewel after jewel came to me as I went thru one stack after another, about sixteen in total. All sorts of data with monthly operating costs, power production and the weirdest of them all, power bought and sold by American Electric Power. One was from one of the country's largest power producers, the TVA.

The biggest gift of all was a map. The E.C.A.R. (East Coast Area Reliability) map that was as big as my double size bed showing all the power lines of 88 Kva and larger all the way up to the biggest 765 Kva lines in the east central power area ranging from Georgia to Canada and all the way from the east coast out to Iowa.

First thing I did was to take out the ECAR map. It had all the existing power generation locations and substations on it. I started with the booklet that had the proposed power generation and power distribution lines projected to be built over the next 20 years. Spreading out the map I maliciously plotted out each new power station and the lines projected from each. Also, there were the proposed lines that ran between existing lines including the one running thru Floyd County. When I got finished with the map the layout was looking like a Chutes and Ladders game with the ladders laid sideways running from east to west with American Electric Power's 765 Kva being the longest line running from the Mississippi River all the way thru southern central Virginia.

Other companies had their monster lines running orientated in an east to west direction to the north and to the south sides of American Electric Power Companies monster line, but they were only 500 Kva lines at the maximum. Each 765 Kva power line can carry about 2.5 times the capacity of a 500 Kva line at normal operation guidelines. Enough to power a mid-sized city like Baltimore. Intermittently spaced between the main backbone of these ladders were rungs going up and down, north and south. This was between the ladder that were laying sideways making a boxed in mosaic. Most of these lines were 500 Kva or less in size. American Electric Power Company's 765 Kva line was the largest and right in the center making it the backbone of the entire power grid. If any of these power lines were cut, power could be routed around with a flip of the switch.

After plotting all the proposed new lines and new power plants I realized that some seemed to be out of place. The 2 proposed lines by Appalachian Power Company including the one running thru Floyd County which also included the future line running from Martinsville to Lynchburg. These lines ran at angles between the rungs of the ladder while most all other connections were mostly straight rungs between the power line ladders. The proposed Appalachian Power Company lines did no specific good as the straight line rungs were the strongest ties between ladders. What this said to me was the two new lines proposed running into Martinsville were not needed if they built only the one line from Martinsville into Matt Funk first only bolstering my original position with the Citizens for the Preservation of Floyd County group. Why build 51 miles of line when you can build 186 miles and get paid more for it.

But, that was not the task at hand. The plotting also produces a new line running into Matt Funk from the northern new generating stations sometime into the future making it a stronger rung like connection. Looking at the finished product it gave me a good oversight as to what they were really doing.

Then came the past operating logs from all the operating arms of American Electric Power. I had to compile each arm into a total consumption package by each month and year. I was then able to plot these on a geometric chart and it showed a straight line growth rate that was fairly consistent year after year with minor spikes and valleys. The problem with this past performance was the growth rate came out to be only 4.0% per year, not the 15.0% yearly growth rate the power company was indicating for the next 20 years.

Then came the spread sheets for the parent company, American Electric Company. What was this about? It took me a while to fully grasp the meaning. I had recently started classes for a Master's Degree in Business and I had just completed the basic required accounting classes. Now my knowledge of engineering and accounting allowed the spread sheets to talk to me in business terms, how to make a profit and do nothing for it. American Electric Power Company was buying excess electric production from other power companies like the TVA, Duke Power and Carolina Power and Light. Why spend money on inefficient fuel production facilities when they bought excess power from the south including the TVA (Tennessee Valley Authority) for as little as $0.02 per kilowatt-hour and sold it to underpowered electric generating companies in the north like Pittsburgh Power and Light and other under producing power companies for $0.05 to $0.065 cents per kilowatt-hour, as much as the market could sustain. And how did they do that? Through their 765 Kva power lines of course of which they were now petitioning the Virginia State Corporation Commission to have the consumer pay for the construction of the new power lines to bring power to other power companies and pay for this program with increased rates and the AFUDC. All that while stating it was needed for the reliability of electric power to the area and we, the consumers had to pay for it. That's great if you can do it. Have the public pay for these lines and their upkeep and rake in millions of profits for power that had nothing to do with Appalachian Power Company production or consumption. No wonder they retained the best attorneys in the state, in Roanoke and in Richmond, the state capitol of Virginia. They had to protect their interests at any cost.

And it just kept getting better. With all the coalfields they owned and with enough coal to last hundreds of years, they were planning the doubling of the coal fired power generation stations over the next 20 years and the same holds true with the new proposed 765 Kva power line construction projects. When I got finished plotting all their projected lines over the next 20 years, things became so clear. The network shouted out they didn't need to build the 72-mile long power line to start with. But if they built it first it would become an unneeded redundancy when the other lines were completed. And that doesn't include the line going from Martinsville to Lynchburg, Va., which was next on their agenda. If they built my 51-mile long power line they would not need either of these proposed line. Just to make it clear, the original filling stated the second phase to Lynchburg was needed and would be scheduled to start just after the first leg was completed. Oh my, oh my, what have just I stepped in to?

One of the things that stood out was the persistent use of cheap power being sold to small underpowered companies to keep them from building new facilities. Point in case was a smaller power company located mainly in south central Ohio that was barely producing enough power to supply the low end of their power usage with old outdated generating facilities. For years and years American Power Company was feeding them underpriced electricity for slightly less than what it cost them to produce. The cost to modernize the plants would require new exhaust scrubbers and environmentally safe facilities that would take years to engineer and construct. By the time they would finish, the amortized cost of the electricity they would produce would exceed the cost they were being charged by American Electric Power

American Electric Power Company was still buying bulk power from other sources far below the ongoing bulk re-sales price. Over the years American Electric Power Company bought their stock and placed some members on their board. They were going to take that power company over I thought to myself. Under the utility antimonopoly rules developed after the stock market crash of 1929, they just couldn't buy the power company outright. The power company had a loophole. They had to prove that they were a vital part of the company and without power being supplied by American Electric Power Company the small company could not properly provide uninterrupted electric power for its customers. My thoughts were that this small company is going to be taken over sometime in the future. A few years late that did come to pass and that little company now collectively called AEP Ohio along with other holdings in Ohio became another jewel assimilated into the American Electric Power Company family. Currently American Electric Power Company owns 10 public utilities companies from east Texas north to Michigan and east to central Virginia.

But what about the A.F.U.D.C.? The allowance for funds used during construction, you know, that thing you didn't know anything about. Well, I researched it as much as I could. It was a pre-tax deduction of

7% of the total money spent for new construction, regardless of what they were building. This money did not need to be earmarked for anything. It could go into a slush fund, king of a grease for a wheel for special patronage maybe. It was free to use as the power company saw fit. Specifically, the more money they spent on construction, the more money they had to use. It was an accounting trick used to bolster their cash position. I believe this accounting procedure was used in the previous construction of its main 765 Kva power transmission lines and they wanted to make it automatic for all new construction projects instead of having to apply for each separate construction project as in the past.

CHAPTER 20:

LET IT SNOW

When quitting time came around at 5 pm, it was lightly snowing. Everybody had been listening to the radio in the office, which was calling for heavy snows after dark. I decided to take the alternate route along the Blue Ridge Parkway. The grades are very gentle but was further away to get to adding 10 miles to my trip home. The road going up the back side of Bent Mountain is the main road going into Floyd. The road is steep and winding with little if anything to stop one from sliding off the side of the mountain. I-81 going up the other side of Bent Mountain only dumps you out at Christiansburg where the roads are narrow, steep and much worse going into Floyd County. I made a dash to the parkway entrance located on the southern side of Roanoke County. The roads were empty and the snow falling gently. I watched a vehicle pull into the parkway entrance right behind me thru my rear view mirror. It was a State Park Ranger and I watched him stop and put down the gate closing the roadway as I drove further up the road. Oh great, that means there's nobody coming behind me over the next 20 miles until morning when the snow plows would come through. The snow was steadily falling gently. It was lightly covering the road and I still had good traction. It was an uneasy quiet with no other vehicles coming or going in either direction. But my old faithful Chevy pick-up truck was doing fine and at steady clip around 30 miles per hour. As I got higher into the mountains, the snow got deeper and deeper. When I reached the crest of Bent Mountain I relaxed as I knew the worst and the steepest parts were over, at least I thought the worst was over.

Then I got to a hollow where the roadbed was filled and raised over 20 feet above the level drainage low below. There were no shoulders on either side of the road. I hit a slick spot in 6+ inches of snow on the road. My rear right traction wheel slid to the right and off the road. I got stuck. It was a steep embankment of over 45 degrees and about a 20 foot deep drop off. There were no cell phones in those days and it was at least 1/2 mile thru the woods and fields needing to trek thru 6 or more inches of snow to a house.

I got out surveying the damage to the vehicle. The drive shaft and gearbox were sitting on the ground at the edge of the embankment and the right rear wheel was dangling free over 6 feet above the ground, it was that steep. I worked my way under the truck almost sliding down to the bottom, but was able to hold onto small trees. I had to wedge my feet between these small tree trunks and the ground just to stand up straight under the wheel. There was nothing I could do from way down here, then I crawled my way back up. The only tool I had with me was a small crank up jack. I put the small jack behind the drive shaft and screwed up the jack to the full extension of the jack. The bumper and rear of the truck were up enough so the wheel and axel were at least even with the other tire on the road. I had to get onto the road and pull the truck bed towards the center of the road. It had to work, if the weight of the truck went the wrong way and the axel shifted to the right, the truck could tumble down the embankment. I braced myself the best I could against the slippery road and pulled. The truck slowly started to move to the left until the jack slipped out. Yes! I got a couple of inches towards the center of the road. But that didn't quite get the drive wheel to the road so I needed to jack it up some more times to push the truck further into the road. I had to do this until the wheel caught the edge of the shoulder. Success, I packed up the jack and drove off as if I hadn't spent the last half hour getting a good workout. The snow kept piling up in front of me yet my trusty stead did get me home with no further incident.

I had the rest of that winter of 1978 to study the information. The hard part was trying to separate data. The only time I had available was mainly on the weekends with some work at night after work. The power company had 2 separate phases of the rate hike. The most important was the cost of new facilities for an over inflated use as they were projecting a growth rate of 15% per year. Plotting graphs of the power usage over the past 20 years, it was more like 4.5%. Then I had to fight the allowance for funds used in construction, a 7% increase from what they already received. The money they got back could go anywhere and I was certain that it would go into a slush fund to grease the hands of high-ranking state officials. It was non-taxable money coming back to them to use as they saw fit. I needed to put on my best thinking cap and see if I could combine the 2 together and still be professional about it.

I had prepared multiple graphs and charts showing the projected rate of growth from Appalachian Power Company's rate request against the historic rate of growth for the past 20 years as supplied by American Electric Power Company. There was nothing extra ordinary about these as they were historical in nature and nothing mind blowing contained within. I guess they didn't feel as if my testimony or presentation of data would affect the rate proceedings in any negative way. Therefore, I believed no contact was made between Appalachian Power Company and Mr. William F. Clark about my upcoming testimony. I didn't have that feeling coming at me from Mr. Clark this time.

CHAPTER 21:

SAVING MONEY

The hearing for the rate increase came up in the spring of 1978 at the State Corporation Commission building in Richmond, Virginia. I had taken that day off as personal vacation time. Art Guepe approved my time off and was fully aware that I was testifying. The attorneys for the power company opened up with their reasoning for the filings and presented the Chief Engineer for American Electric Power Company as their main witness. He was quite comfortable and very confident on the stand and stated the facts as necessary to strengthen the rate increase case for Appalachian Power Company. He didn't say anything spectacular, just generalities about being prudent but still having new power available for any growth spurts in the coming years.

After his testimony the court heard from other interested parties. I asked Struther as to when I would be presenting my testimony to the Commission. He said I was last. We were to be the last in a long line of people who didn't want the rate increase. Hours of listening to them and they would not get to hear my testimony. It was all for show as they could not present any good reasoning as to why the rates should not be raised for future construction. They were just letting off steam and the attorneys for the power company just sat by and smiled as there was nothing that could affect the rate increase proposal presented by any of these Protestants. Finally, the last of the Protestants finished and our time had come.

S. Strother Smith III got up and talked about how the rate increase was going to hurt the people of southwest Virginia. Then he introduced me as the expert witness. I had a number of graphs with me and explained how I reached the conclusions in my report. I had proved without a doubt using standard accepted actuarial principals that no rate increase was needed at this time or in the foreseeable future for projected growth in Appalachian Power Company's service area. At that time we were in an economic recession of sorts to boot. When Strother got finished asking me questions I still felt like I needed to get something in about the route of no route. The one I had testified against 2 years earlier as wasteful spending for redundancy construction that was the heart of this rate hike. Strother had told me that rules could only allow me to answer direct questions from the Commission or the power company attorneys if they so inquired. We took a little break, I told Strother I needed to get these things in. He told me he could not ask me the question I needed in order to bring these items into the hearing as they were not part of our pre-trial package submitted to the power company a few weeks earlier. That would seal the reasoning for lowering the rate increase for construction costs if he could only get me in.

This hearing wasn't about the previous construction program, just the proposed growth rate throughout the region and the need for prudent growth now instead of later in the future when construction costs would be so much higher. I felt stymied. I knew I could win only if I could open the eyes of the commission to the wasteful and greedy wants of the power company. Would my testimony be enough? From looking at the commissioners and the attorneys for the power company, I felt that it would not be enough. Everyone appeared to be complacent even after my graphs proved they didn't need the rate increase. There just wasn't enough to turn the tide away from the power company. This rate increase was in the bag for the power company just as long as they were able to keep me quiet.

When we returned I got back on the witness stand. It was the power company attorney's turn to cross-examine me. It was also the power company's attorney's job to play down the importance of my testimony and to play me as a small town engineer with no expertise in running a power company or understanding it's needs. Just the usual questions, place of work, current address, a lack of anything important. I'm sitting there saying to myself, ask the question, just ask any question that gives me the right to introduce new evidence into the hearing. Just ask it please!

I could only wish that the attorneys felt a little unsure about my previous testimony. Edgy enough that maybe it might, in some fashion, carry some weight and make them feel as if they needed more to discredit me. Just as I thought the attorney was going to wrap it up, he asked me about my expertise as a witness as I had not worked for a power company and was just a lowly county civil engineer? Did he not know that the State Corporation Commission had already approved me as an expert witness?

That's it. "What gives you the knowledge to think you know more about power production than the chief engineer?" Or, something very close to that. My heart started to race and I began to explain how the power company was needlessly spending money on projects not needed, building about 175 miles of power line when only 51 miles would do. Collecting A.F.U.D.C. on every penny they spent building new lines. The attorney for the power company tried to stop this as introduction of new material not compatible to the proceedings at hand. The head commissioner just leered at him sideways and said he had "opened the door with this question. Now you have to let him speak."

I went through this in a whirl and I can't even remember what I said or when I got off the stand. I do remember getting into the testimony the vast amount of money American Power Company was making selling cheap power generated by other over electric producing companies and selling it to other under producing power companies at double or more the cost. They were able to do this by transmitting it over lines paid for by the consumers and bypassing the individual operating companies books to make it look like they weren't making much money. I was shaking for some time after I got finished. Just getting off the stand and out the door was like walking in an earthquake. The hearing was then officially over and I had gotten in all the information I wanted to, I thought. Strother said I did, but I was still shaking, teeth clanging together and nodded in return to his statements as we left the building on the way to the parking lot. Now the cat was out of the bag and it was time to go back home. I could not speak a word as my mouth muscles were tightened up so much. All the information supplied by the power company was used to its full capacity against it.

A week or more passed and I got busy back at work. Then, one day I heard on the radio on my way back home from Roanoke that the request for the rate hike for construction was denied and only $20 million was awarded for minor cost of fuel price relief. The power company just lost over $144,000,000 per year for the next 20 years with this defeat that would have been a shoe in if I had not gotten all of my testimony in. I was happy on the way back home knowing that I, going solo, could make a difference against a well-oiled machine hell bent to succeed at any cost.

The very next day while walking up the stairs, Mr. Clark was coming down the stairs. When he spotted me his face turned cherry red. His cheeks puffed as if he were holding his breath maybe trying to keep from saying anything to me. I could feel his anger penetrating deep into me. It froze me in my tracks as he focused his eyes upon me while passing me. I thought I saw steam coming ears, but it was just an illusion from the lighting in the stairwell. From that minute on I know I was a dead duck as an employee of Roanoke County and needed to find another job or source of income soon.

CHAPTER 22:

BACK TO SCHOOL

There was pressure on me to do something. I needed to get a new job someplace as working there at this time was untenable. Mr. Clark and his ill will towards me was constantly on my mind. Unfortunately, we were in the grips of a double digit inflation and the Vietnam War was recently ended. Roanoke County was not giving full cost of living increases, just step increases and a small cost of living increase totaling about 6% per year during 12% – 18% inflation times. Engineering jobs were hitting the skids, but I was keeping my limited options available.

During this elapsed time I got a call from my Veterans Administration representative. I didn't know I had a VA representative. He said time is running out on my VA benefits and this office has plenty of funds not used. If I went back to school I could go for my master's degree. Under the G.I. plan I could get up to $444.00 per month which was way more than my tuition would be. In order to get this amount I would have to be a full time student.

Since I was mustered out of the service in April of 1969, I had until April 1979 before the funding ran out to get my Master's Degree. I signed up for summer classes in late spring of 1978 and started back to full time day and evening classes going to Roanoke County Community College during my lunch hour 5 days a week and 2 more classes every night to keep me at 12 hours so I could be considered full time and make up necessary classes.

This way I would also have the necessary undergraduate courses necessary to qualify for graduate studies in the School of Business. This way I could go for a Master's Degree in the fall and still collect $444.00 per month, and graduate in May of 1979. This was a blessing. I breezed thru the accounting classes and starting business classes maintaining a high B to a low A average while working full time at the county engineering office. Art Guepe helped to push my decision to go back to school too. There was a 5 hour course offered at 12:00 that fit perfectly into my work schedule. Yes, I was late a few times getting back from lunch, but that couldn't hurt my performance ratings which were already down in the dumps as far as Mr. Clark was concerned. During that summer I took a Real Estate class as the only available elective in order to keep my hours at 12 or more. I passed the Real Estate class and qualified to take the Real Estate licensing exam, which I took and passed easily.

Another intervention in my behalf came my way as the Dean of Admissions at Radford College was also in a similar faith group and was a neighbor to my wife's aunt. In reviewing my grades from Virginia Tech, they were not the best. Some would say they sucked but they let me into the new school of graduate learning from my past work history and military service. I guess I was filling and empty quota slot. That has its benefits and I was accepted on probation for 1 quarter. I learned new study habits quickly. I curled up in the kitchen at the end of the dining area with my back to the raised pot belly style wood stove. That stove was on all the time during my endless hours of studies over the winter. Many times the warmth relaxing me so much I would fall asleep at the dining table long after everyone else was sound asleep. For my efforts I did manage to get a B in insurance and actuary tables. But the rest were A's. I was no longer on probation and continued night classes.

CHAPTER 23:

WOOLY BULLY

One thing about living on a farm is the high degree of self-reliability we get into in order to sustain our family. We would plant the outside 2 rows of our cornfield with sweet corn and that would give us hundreds of ears of white and yellow cross pollinated sugar corn, we would freeze whole ears, cut the kernels off the cob and freeze them or give the excess to or neighbors. You could always tell when it was harvest time; the kitchen would be full of empty mason jars as it was that time of year to put away your garden for the winter. Fall was always a time of bounty and one neighbor or another would have a bountiful harvest and share with the others, like the apple butter making ceremony where we would stand around a huge kettle of boiling apples and talk and take turns stirring the pot, and when it was all cooked, we got to fill a few dozen mason jars with the best apple butter money could buy. But, then, who buys apple butter anyway?

The whole family would go out behind the house with empty gallon milk jugs and fill them up with huckleberries growing behind the house on the gentle downside of the hill. Sometimes we ate more than we put into the jugs I think. But, that wasn't all we put away. We had cattle, and that year we put away our first-born male young bull, Wooly Bully. He was a very friendly young bull and the children would always go out and pet him when the herd came around. After a while he got large enough where our resident bull no longer looked at him as a child, but a rival and we decided to ship him to the local butcher shop. The next week he came back nicely wrapped and labeled. That night Ginny made a big roast and put it in the middle of the table. Ginny and I picked on it for a while, but the kids couldn't stomach it. We learned that it was easier to make ground beef meat sauce to start until they got used to the idea of eating off the land. Now, I would be remiss if I didn't tell about my baking. I got to be quite good at making yeast-bread, mostly different rye and wheat mixes with fennel and caraway seeds. The smell would fill the house and when they came out of the oven, there was a line waiting for me to slice the warm bread and slap on the butter.

CHAPTER 24:

SETTING THE HOOK

If you want to catch a big fish, you need a big hook. Then you have to properly set the hook to keep it from getting away. I had told Art Guepe that I was only going to sell real estate on weekends only and I would only sell farms and acreage tracts and I would concentrate my efforts in Floyd County. But, I didn't know that there were no active Real Estate offices in Floyd county. All the Real Estate offices selling land in Floyd County were located in Roanoke County. So, I put my license with a broker known to do land sales in Floyd County.

I subsequently listed a large tract of land, an old farm, at the base of Bent Mountain. I had known the owner and he wanted me to list his farm as he trusted me. I got a full price offer from another Broker who specialized in land speculation. He told me he was trying to buy this land from the farmer for over a year. We went to contract with an all cash offer. Just before settlement he met me at the farm and said he wanted not just his commission but all my commission as well or he was going to tell the County Administrator that I was making promises about subdividing the property, which I wasn't. It was either give up your commission or you could lose your job. I didn't care for this person and the commission was being paid to the Broker of the company I worked for, not to me so I couldn't give it up.

As a result of this he went directly to Mr. Clark and made allegations about my dealings and that I as county engineer would have more and unfair knowledge about Real Estate sales. He may have even lied by saying I was making promises for subdivision approvals. Mr. Clark responded by writing a letter of understanding on January 30, 1979 that set forth a number of new restrictions on my actions as a Real Estate agent. In order to keep me from having an appearance of impropriety I was not allowed to sell houses or subdivided lots in Roanoke County. I agreed to that as I wasn't selling those to begin with. I even said I would give up my Real Estate license if that was what was needed to keep my name above board from any suspicion of double dealings. He required me to sign off on the letter that I concurred. Some things in the letter were not true, but when your boss confronts you with this knowing that if I didn't concur, he would have fired me then and there for failure to follow a direct order.

I then removed my Real Estate license from being active and gave up selling Real Estate anywhere in Virginia. There was an uneasy truce for the next few months between Mr. Clark and myself. He knew he modified my agreement way beyond the parameters of which I had originally obtained my license and then he pulled the strings tight.

CHAPTER 25:

HOLD ON

One morning in March I arriving at work. I could feel a pall over the building, the walls stared at me as if to say something bad was going to happen. I went to my office and there was dead silence. The secretary wouldn't even raise her head when I said good morning, just silence. It wasn't until about noon when Art came to my office and told me I was being fired for violation of County Policy, the terms were to be spelled out at later date. I knew it was going to happen, I had known for years it was going to happen. Just the right kicker was needed.

I called Strother Smith, he told me to immediately file a request for arbitration. That I did over the next few days. Then the fun began. I needed to pick someone from my side, the county picks someone from their side and those two have to meet in the middle and pick a 3rd arbitrator. Strother chose his own friend as our panel member of whom I knew nothing. Roanoke County chose another county administrator from an adjacent county. Strother had known about this person, a retired state trooper known for his stern handling of county employees. We had a week to come up with additional names. Each side would submit 5 additional names and the 3rd panel member would come from that list. Strother picked four prominent names from local business. I picked one name of a person my wife and I had met through our faith based group experience, Eddy. It came down to a short list, their pick and our pick, Eddy. We were out of it and had nothing else to do with the selection process. At that time Eddy lived in another county on the other side of Roanoke where the opposing arbitrator and County Administrator chosen by Roanoke County was from. Apparently the Roanoke County Attorneys didn't he didn't have much faith in their last name on their list, and Eddy was a personnel manager at a local company and was familiar with arbitrations. They chose Eddy as the 3rd panel member, not our side. Not that Eddy owed us anything, I just knew he would do the right thing. And doing the right thing meant everything as far as I was concerned.

It was well over a week or more before the hearing began. Both attorneys held preliminary testimony for discovery purposes. They used the fact that I had acquired a real estate license during my time that I went to college and I went to classes during work hours as reason for dismissal. I had answered questions by stating Art Gueppe allowed me to get the license and he was aware that my accounting classes ran from 12:00 noon to 12:45 PM and I used my lunch hour to attend these classes. That, in the year that I had a license I worked on weekends only a sold only one piece of land during that time. The arbitration began with deposition testimony being read into the records. I noticed they had a new attorney presenting for Roanoke County in addition to Mr. Ed Natt.

Apparently they were trying to get as far away from people that knew me. This was an attorney with experience in these matters, the county wanted to make sure I didn't get off the hook. I explained that the license was obtained after the evening Real Estate class I had taken as an elective. I had to get in the extra hours to keep my full time standing for the Veterans Administration money. Also, that I qualified to take the exam for real estate licensure by passing the course. And I did not think anything about it. When I passed the exam I told Art Guepe, my direct supervisor and he had no problem with real estate on the weekends. Also, it was common knowledge that over 10% of all county employees had real estate licenses to help supplement the meager salary of a southern county employees. And, as for going to class during county time, that was totally false. The college was only a few miles down the main road from the courthouse and I would get to the accounting class 5 minutes late and still be back at the office by 1 PM.

There was a new charge that I was totally unaware of. The county was saying that I had reduced a contractor's performance bond for a Realtor that I did business with. I didn't know what they were talking about nor which sub-development they were referring to. In their allegations I had reduced a bond below what was necessary to complete the final paving section and there wasn't enough money left to complete the paving fully. Now, I need to make one thing perfectly clear. My job was to go out and identify all work completed and estimate the remaining work to complete the infrastructure which included paving, sewer and water lines, drainage, curbs and sidewalks and street lighting and street signs.

I had reviewed many developments over the years. The procedure that was in place was as follows: A builder would make a request thru the Roanoke County Board of Supervisors and Mr. William F. Clark to release part of the bond once substantial work was completed. That was then sent to Art Guepe who had the authority to release all or part of the performance bond. Art would give me the plans and I would go out and make a list of the work completed and work needed to finish the project. Using the numbers from the original bond, Art would come up with a maximum value to be released based upon my field inspection. Then I would write up a letter to Art with the numbers for his review. If approved by Art, it was then sent to the developer for reduction of funds. Now in all my time reviewing bonds they could only come up with one incident where there wasn't enough money left to complete all of the improvements should the developer walk away from the project. And who's fault was that. I didn't set the value of the performance bond, Art Guepe did, along with the design engineers at the value of work at the time of submittal.

They went into deliberation and decision didn't come down until the next day. All three of three arbitrators agreed that Roanoke County wasn't justified to fire and employee for a minor offense that was archaic in nature and that the county didn't give the employee any opportunity to remedy the infraction in written notification, no prior warning. Even the Roanoke County hand-picked chosen arbitrator agreed with the final findings. Also that I had done nothing inappropriate in the performance bond reduction. I was ordered back to work the next Monday with past pay due in full. I knew my days were numbered with the county when I got back to work. I didn't know just how low that number really was.

That day I arrived back, I was told to wait outside the attorney's office and wait I did. I waited and I waited for what was to be hours. The county attorney, Mr. Ed Natt brought me an envelope and said you can't come back to work. Your position has been filled with another engineer. Oh my God. Oh my God. What am I going to do? I had three children and a wife to support. My daughter Susan was now 2.

Since I was fired I knew it would be impossible to get unemployment insurance and I had already received my last VA check for Graduate School. First thing I did was run down to the unemployment office anyway and file a claim. It would take a week to determine my eligibility. When I returned to the unemployment office next week the county had opposed the issuance of unemployment on grounds for dismissal. I had to go to the unemployment supervisor's office as they reviewed the case.

The county's case for dismissal was in writing, I had to give my side to the supervisor. After a thorough review, they did allow unemployment insurance payments, which also indicated the weakness of the counties firing proceedings. In those days you could not get unemployment insurance if your employer contested the application for unemployment insurance for just cause.

Graduation day finally came. I had earned my Masters Degree in Business Administration with a minor in Economics. As it turned out I was number 2 in the graduating master's program. A teacher that only took 1 class per quarter and four full years to get a perfect 4.0 GPA. My 3.94 GPA seemed to be meaningless to me. When I went up for my degree they handed me a box along with my diploma and another scroll. I looked at the box after I took my seat; it was a gold key and membership to Delta Mu Delta National Honor Society. That was a surprise. However, that didn't put any additional meat on the table.

CHAPTER 26:

THE DEPRESSING DAYS

I had made a resume and sent it out to all job openings within 100 miles of my house and many others over 100 miles away, but never heard back from any of them over the next 6 months. So many fit within my qualifications, but not a word. It got so bad that my wife let me know that she wanted a divorce and constantly sang the popular country song lyrics D-I-V-O-R-C-E to me every time she gave me my supper. The children thought it was funny, but they didn't know what was really going on. On the days that I had nowhere to go and little to do she didn't want to be left alone with me. When the kids were in school she would leave me at home alone reading want ads, working around the house and generally feeling bad for myself. Sex was a non-issue, don't ask as you won't get any anyway. I was just about totally broken by that time in the middle of the summer.

We were running out of money and had less than a month of unemployment insurance left. Late that summer the call came in. The Dean of the Radford College graduate business school had called me at home. He said he had spoken to the President of Wytheville Community College. They had an opening for an assistant business professor. He recommended me very highly stating I was the best student he ever had in all his years as a business professor at Yale, or maybe it was Harvard, I can't remember which. The job was mine, no questions asked and the starting pay was $15,600 per year. A meager salary to start that was close to what I was making at Roanoke County, but a salary nonetheless. We were saved. But, I was afraid of this job. I knew I could make a good teacher, but the thought of facing a classroom full of young adult students was terrifying.

But, before I could accept that job, another call came in from The Dravo Corporation. They wanted to meet me right away if I was still available. They paid for the airplane tickets flying from Roanoke to Pittsburgh, Pennsylvania and return. I flew up there; they liked my previous construction background. They also told me the report from Roanoke County was so poor that they could see right thru it. It didn't take long and they offered me the job which was building a new coal preparation plant and railroad facility in Toms Creek, Virginia, 120 miles due west of my home. The kicker was they were paying $29,000 per year and I was to be a subcontractor and they would also pay my expenses. I was to start as soon as I could get there, next week at the latest. I said I would love to, but I needed to speak with my wife first. She agreed, we needed the money and it got me away from the house which was good for her for a week at a time. I also needed a place to stay and found a nice sized camper for sale, but we needed cash. I was a tenured employee at Roanoke County and had some funds built up for retirement. I cashed it in the next day and bought the camping trailer for cash, then towed it down behind the pick-up truck to Toms Creek which was an old defunct mining town about 3 miles north of Coeburn, Virginia.

The construction site was on a lonely stretch of uninhabited road surrounded by mountains rising up to 2,000 feet higher than the plant. Scars encircled every visible mountain face where modern day strip-mining operations were performed. It was a strange and different environment and the nights were lonely and cold. Dravo had brought in an office trailer with map tables and drawers. I set up my camper about 50 feet away from the office. The site contractor previously hired by Dravo had already begun stripping vegetation. There was no wasting of time, I had to jump in and there was no turning back. The next week we had our first meeting with my superiors of Dravo and the ANR Coal Company, the owners. Introductions were made and the scope of my work, which was everything I needed to be doing, was formally stated. Usually this is a 2 or 3 man job site, but I was the team, going solo again. My job was to schedule the subcontractors, supervise the work and make sure proper quality of materials and testing were performed, record progress and make on the spot changes to the plans that I found necessary. This was a design build company and that was what I was doing. After the meeting they said all went well, but they had only one complaint. I answered the questions too quickly. They suggested that I smoke a pipe as it would slow my responses down and give me the appearance I was deeply thinking about the problems at hand. I had quit smoking 10 years earlier as my mother had died from smoking with lung and stomach cancer as did many of my other aunts and uncles.

As I was getting started, S. Strother Smith III was putting together a filing in the U.S. 4th District Circuit Court in Roanoke. During this time I had little contact with him except for an occasional bill for expenses. The only time I had at home was on the weekends and I spent the time with my children, I didn't have bedroom privileges. I slept on the couch and my 3-year-old daughter would not let me out of her sight. She would fall asleep next to me every night I was home. Then I would carry her to her room and lay her down with a kiss when I got sleepy, but always returning to the couch. She tough me the true meaning of unconditional love. My relationship with my wife seemed to be getting better. Later that fall I asked her to get a baby sitter for the night and come down to Abingdon where we could have a quiet diner for just the 2 of us and a romantic night at a bread and breakfast. Without taking time to think about it, she refused. At that time I knew it was over. She was only nicer because we had some money and the pressure to pay bills was no longer putting pressure on us.

Late that fall we were invited to the annual holiday's party at Tom and his wife's house in the middle of the Town of Floyd. This was a large post Victorian era 2 story and was originally owned by his grandfather who was the county doctor. Tom always loved to tell the story about his grandfather, or maybe it was his great grandfather. This was in the days before the horseless carriage. Taking the horse pulled carriage to the ailing families home throughout Floyd County and returning in the wee hours of the morning many times falling asleep on the way back. But, the horse knew the way back and he would wake up in the morning in the barn. Being the prominent citizen of Floyd that he was, he was the first one to get a horseless carriage and was proud of it, but he was getting older. One day after a long night of a doctoring visit he fell asleep driving home and became the first (maybe) auto casualty in Floyd County. When we got to the party, Ginny went in first and mingled by herself amongst the women. I tried to follow, but ended up with the men folk in the kitchen who were marveling about the moonshine Tom had gotten and they were drinking it out of mason jars. One must remember that the area between Franklin and Floyd Counties was the moonshine capitol of Virginia during the prohibition era. Marveling at the clarity and the bead, a slow moving air bubble. They passed the jar around, When it got to me I took a small sip. I didn't like it and didn't take anymore. It was just too strong for me, all 180 proof. I felt like a stranger amongst friends. They all knew something was wrong with my marriage and they avoided that conversation about my problems like the plague. Felling alone and down, I decided to go over to my wife. I walked up her from the rear and put my arm around her waist. She grabbed my wrist and pushed it away from her in front of the other women. That was it, rejection in front of friends. What could say it louder. She didn't want to be with me anymore. All hope of resurrecting this marriage went out the window at that moment.

CHAPTER 27:

DARK NIGHTS AHEAD

I had been kidding myself all along. I was now sure that our marriage was over. As the nights got longer and the winter nights got really cold, I couldn't get to sleep without crying about the loss of my family, especially my daughter. I started drinking to dull the senses. It took a half a quart of Jim Bean every night to fall asleep all winter long and I became a wreck waiting on a train. I was burying myself in my work, working deep into the night, keeping myself busy just to help keep my mind off my marriage.

10 years of marriage going down the drain. College sweethearts, I can remember the first day we met. I said to myself, that's the girl I'm going to marry. And I did. But now something came between us. She was embarrassed to be with me because of losing my job and being fired in a public way. All this happened because I had tried to help my neighbors? Was that right? Where did all that love go? I was so alone. Nobody that I knew from work, church, and socially tried to contact me or have conversations with me. My marriage going down the tubes. This job was all I had left.

Chapter 28:

RUN FOR YOUR LIFE

Come next spring, the job was running very well and I knew I had to do something about my drinking. After quitting time the area became deathly silent except for an occasional vehicle passing. But, the hills started calling me, run Ricky run. I hadn't run since my army days. I drove my vehicle up an access ramp behind my trailer to the lower strip-mining plateau and marked off ½ mile from the office. I had my mind made up that I was going to run 1 mile a day. My first try I didn't make it up the ramp without having to stop, and then on the flat area, stop, start, stop, start on and on until I reached the marker I had set and returned about an hour later. I was determined to do this. I didn't have much else to do at night as the daylight hours were getting longer. I started to run every evening before diner. After a few weeks I was able to go all the way to the ½ mile marker and back without stopping and eventually my legs stopped burning. This did help by making me tired after running and I slowly stopped drinking and could fall asleep much faster. I began to feel better about myself and started to set new goals for running. First 1 mile every night, then 2, then a little more. By that summer I was in very good condition and set my sights on the road in front of the trailer.

I had run to the base of the steep slope many times before. The acrid stench from the water discharged from the old mines would fill my nose. But it was worth the exercise. I was determined to conquer the mountain. That night I would make it up the hill or bust. When I started I had to go a mile and a half uphill at a slight uphill grade to a sharp break in the gradient where the grade increased to 10% and more in places. The top of the mountain was more than 2,800 feet in elevation while Toms Creek was at 2,000 feet. On this summer night I said I was going to go all the way uphill. I ran and I ran and it hurt so bad my steps were like tippy toe steps at the steepest parts, my heart was beating so hard I felt like the sides of my neck and the top of my head were going to explode, and I was sweating so much the salty water poured off my head into my eyes and I couldn't see the road in front of me. I was almost ready to turn around when I reached the little country store at the top of the hill, the 4 mile mark. I had put a dollar in my little back pocket and bought a cold soda of which I could hardly drink, but I did. After cooling down, it was 4 miles back to the trailer and that was a cool running with my arms flailing around in the breeze I kicked up. I was moving so fast I could hardly get my feet in front of me. But, something else happened that happened that evening that at first seemed quite odd. A woman driving by honker her car horn and whistled at me.

CHAPTER 29:

SEXUAL HEALING

That summer something else happened to me that would once again change my life forever. A young woman recently graduated from a local community college in environmental sciences came to the job side. She was the new water sample taker for the environmental testing sub-contractor. This was necessary to make sure the ground water wasn't getting polluted from our ground altering operations. She needed to pull water samples from pita tubes throughout the site. She checked into the site trailer so I could record her presence into the daily log as I did for every weekly visit by the testing company. She was tall, at least 5 foot 8 and thin looking in her kakis. Her MSHA (mine safety) helmet and safety glasses made her look like an old school teacher. One day I was very sick with the flu. The flu didn't stop me from working alone in the trailer as I didn't need to have much contact. It was late in the day and I waived her onto the site and entered her presence into the daily log. On the way out she stopped by and seeing that I was sick, offered me some medicine with honey and hot soup to fix me up. She insisted, it was only a mile or so away. I usually didn't take medicine on my own, so I accepted. I closed down the trailer and followed her to her place.

My head was fuzzy, my temperature high and back muscles really sore. She did what she said and got me a hot medicine drink and bowl of soup. I was sitting at the left side of her couch and she asked me if I was feeling any better. Of course I said no, I felt terrible, nose running and eyes red. Afterwards she walked behind the couch began to deeply rub my back, which nobody had done like this for me before. It felt so good and the medications were starting to work so I started drifting off. Then she opened my shirt and applied menthol-rubbing ointment. My head went back and I really started to drift off even more. I felt so relaxed, she was being so nice to me. Before I could get my senses back her hand drifted down into my pants and pulled out my penis, jumped over me and quickly sat on it. Before I could react, she wasn't wearing underwear either, she had put me deep inside her. But that felt so good, so much better than I remember feeling with my wife. And then it was over. I was still sitting on the couch in a laid back way. I just couldn't say a thing. I felt so used, it was date rape and I felt bad about it, really bad. Did she put something in my medicine? But, I still felt good having had real sex for what may have been years. I pulled my pants the rest of the way up back and tucked in my shirt. There was no kissing involved and I certainly didn't feel obligated to thank her for her services. I was confused and didn't say much in leaving.

What have I done? What have I done? My moral fibers had been compromised. My thoughts ran from I had done something horrible to she did something horrible. Also, thoughts that this would ruin my already broken relationship with Ginny to that it was great sex and I really needed this. My mind was so confused. It was just an isolated incident, would it really hurt anybody if this were to never happen again? If I didn't say anything nobody at home would know, only me.

A few days later she stopped by the office trailer after work. Without speaking a word she looked straight at me, took off her helmet and let her hair down. Then she gave me a kiss and began to touch me, and this time I responded and it was so good. She told me to stop by her home after work. I smiled and nodded, I guess I said I would be there. There was excitement running thru my body again.

Excitement I hadn't felt in years, anticipation of actually being wanted by someone. When I got there she didn't waste any time. She kissed me and started to take her clothes off. She was proud of her body. She had a really good body, tall, thin, and medium breasted. When she wasn't wearing required safety gear, she was quite attractive with long brown hair. The only time I got to see Ginny naked was when I walked into the bathroom while she was in the shower. This was so much better. I couldn't take my eyes off her. Having sex with her got better and better, but I didn't love her, I just wanted her, I just wanted sex. I spent most spare evenings with her for the next few months. She was getting very serious about this relationship and I knew I had to break it off. I still wasn't ready to give up on my family just yet. She kept this going for a while and I couldn't refuse. It felt sooo good to be wanted by someone again.

During this relationship I began to realize that I had been punishing myself all these years for my wife not wanting me sexually as being my fault, my fault because I would hurt her at times. I thought it was my inability to satisfy her, to turn her on and my selfish desire to have a climax. We were in a separation period at that time so was I really cheating. After a few months I ended this relationship as she was getting too deeply involved and I didn't feel as she did. The flip side of this affair was from that time on, the women in the area knew I was in play. I didn't have to go looking for a woman as they seemed to find me wherever I went. Maybe it wasn't that they were looking for me specifically, but my eyes were now open and looking back.

CHAPTER 30:

SAME JOB, DIFFERENT LOCATION

As the job was winding down I was glad to be leaving. Enough is enough. While there, I was the strange for the local women. I thought I could get away from the women. My contract was only for the Toms River job. Dravo Corporation offered another stint, another coal mine job, but this time I got a motel room. I sold my trailer and moved up the road. I hoped I had gotten all this out of my system. I was then shifted to another smaller jobsite in Robinson Creek, Kentucky, about 40 miles further away doing the design work from the start this time. The new job site was about 15 miles south of Pikeville, Kentucky, home of the annual Hatfield and McCoy festival. This was a mini Marti Gras for the area for a weekend, but family oriented. I was officially made a member of clan 3. People collect clan numbers here somewhat like collecting beads at Marti Gras. There is some drinking, but mostly dancing in the streets and fine country food. Don't ask what it was made of, just enjoy.

The people that live here are good hard working folk and coal is king. If your able bodied, you'll probably work in the coal mines. It's a dangerous profession, yet the only way a man can earn a decent way of life for his family. While in my short stay at this location 8 miners were killed in an explosion underground. That mine was just a few hollows away from Robinson Creek. I actually went to an active mine site while at Toms Creek. The mine company representative asked if I wanted to go inside. That site has a coal seam of only 36 inches maximum height. When I got to the front face of the mine, I had to bend way down to see inside. I couldn't do it. It was too closed in there for me. It was claustrophobic. The miners do this every day and have nowhere to stand up until the shift is over. That takes a special kind of person and I take my hat off to them.

After the job was over I had a few weeks off and told my wife we should try and get back together, I still loved her, and I never stopped. That didn't work. Dravo Corporation offered me a full time job as a project manager in a period where they had just laid off 3,500 engineers and employees. They made a spot for me and gave me a project set to start in a few months. But after one month, the project was canceled due to the poor economy. They had one more spot to put me. A steel rolling mill plant in Sonora, Mexico. It had an American family camp with schools and housing, no men without their families allowed. I told Ginny it would be great for the kids and for us. The kids could learn a second language, the pay is fantastic and it would only be for 2 years. If successful there I would be set with the company. She said no, so I had to leave Dravo Corporation to find gainful employment once again. I relocated into New Jersey where there was still work and major construction companies had to have an engineer on every project. I bounced around from job to job going home to see the kids every month or so. I didn't date at all during this time but the final separation papers were signed.

CHAPTER 31:

THE TRIAL

In 1983 I got word that the 4th District Circuit Court in Roanoke was ready to hear the trial. I was working in Atlantic City on the Ocean Club foundation and utility package and foundation work for an addition to the Atlantic City Hospital. Work was very soft, there were many qualified out of work engineers looking for my kind of work position. I got permission to take off for the trial, but only two days. It was early April if I remember correctly. Monday was the first day of the trial. My wife and I met with Strother an hour before the trial was to start. He informed me that he filed this as a Civil Rights discrimination case. He stated that usually, if won the plaintiff was usually awarded 1 dollar in damages and attorney costs. We were asking for $65,000 direct damages plus attorney's costs. He warned me that if we won, and that was a long shot, not to expect anywhere near that amount. Discrimination is difficult to prove especially when the defendants, Roanoke County, claim mal or misfeasance at work and damages are harder to prove. I went in with a heavy heart. Why didn't he file this as another less difficult case to prove lawsuit.

I looked around the courtroom while walking down the center isle. I didn't recognize anybody. Then I realized the county attorneys weren't there, only Mr. Clark from the county was sitting on the left side with 3 new attorneys that I never saw before. When they introduced themselves to the court, Strother told me they were from Woods – Rogers, the law firm retained by Appalachian Power Company. They were doing this pro bono. Oh, oh, oh, I could feel the life within me oozing out the door. These are the best attorneys money could buy, and they were representing Roanoke County gratis, for free just to put me away once and for all. Strother just patted me on the shoulder and said we will get thru it. Answer the questions truthfully and as simply as possible.

As the first day got started it was fairly straightforward. I looked at the jury selected and it was 7 women and 5 men, well-dressed and mixed in ethnic backgrounds. I was on the stand first and the power company attorney's asked about the job, about the firings, the personal time I spent with the citizens group. In the opening arguments the opposition took time laying grounds for dismissal. These were the same arguments made during the arbitration hearing in 1979. They were trying to make it as if I wasn't hurt by the firing, now making over $40,000 per year. They contended that I had erred in my employee duties with the Roanoke County. The first day wrapped up and it didn't go well. They tell you not to look at the jury during testimony, I tried not to, but I saw the lackluster looks on their faces and I knew I did not impress them at all.

The second day came and Mr. Clark was on the stand in the morning. I could tell that he was uncomfortable. I felt a great uneasiness within him. I guess that it in some way made me feel more at ease. The defense attorneys tried to turn the facts around as if I were the one persecuting him. That I instigated ill feelings and ill will, that I deliberately worked on the power company projects on company time and covered it up. That I constantly abused my duties and took off time to go to school when I should be working. Whatever they could think of as to make Mr. Clark seem justified in his actions and the firing. I felt as if Mr. Clark didn't totally agree with the arguments laid forth by the defense.

Lunch break came and Strother let me know that the trial was proceeding somewhat as he expected. Then it was my turn for final rebuttals. Strother asked me for incidents where Mr. Clark showed animosity against me. Besides the first firing for testifying in Floyd County at night, the next strongest was the day after the rate hearing case decision when Mr. Clark passed me in the hall and his face got red as a beet and he looked as if he was biting his tongue not to say something to me. Then it was Appalachian Power Companies attorneys turn to cross-examine me. Again I say Appalachian Power Company as they were doing this for the county, not The County of Roanoke attorneys. They came at me with everything they had, accusing me of things that weren't true, making me falter in my answers as the questions got more and more ambiguous that were sometimes unanswerable. I had to stop my answers many times as I couldn't answer them the way I wanted and answer their questions. I was falling into their trap. All was lost when I glanced a look at the jury. They were not impressed, the power company attorneys were doing their job well. It looked as if we were going to lose this one.

As they were summing it up they began to argue that I was unforthcoming with many of my answers and that I was concealing a motive, why hadn't I answered or stated about my Real Estate dealings, the exact question alludes me. They were putting all their animosity against me making it all came down to this one point. They were so adamant about this that the attorney was pounding his fist against the table to get everyone's attention, especially the jury's. But, I do remember that I answered that question in the prior interrogatories. Yes, I answered it, I told the attorney. I blurted out that I had properly answer that question, it is on page 51 of the interrogatory manuscript.

Everything stopped. Dead silence for a few long moments, then the fluttering of pages. If it wasn't there as I said on that page, then I was a liar at my own doing. After a long moment they found it, on page 51 and carried onto page 52, and I had answered just it as I had said all along.

As they read it aloud to the court you could feel the tide rushing in, the jury was sitting at the edge of their seats listening to every word. The defense attorneys conferred, then said "no more questions". I looked back and forth swinging my head to the jury, the judge, the opposing bench. Then Strother signaled me to come down. It's over, court adjourned for the day. The damage was done! A self-inflicted mortal gunshot by the defense attorney staff. Strother came up to me as we walked out of the courthouse, "how did you know that exact page?" "It just came to me. I saw the page clearly in my mind with the number on the bottom of the page."

Ginny dropped me at the airport for the 6:30 pm flight back to New Jersey. My stomach was in knots all the way back to New Jersey. I didn't know what to think. The next morning I wasn't there as I only had 2 days off. The jury was given its instructions by the judge and then sequestered to deliberate. After 20 minutes the foreman had a question that needed to be clarified and the jury was seated.

My wife called my at the office trailer that afternoon and told me they said. "Your Honor, is the jury allowed to award more money than the Plaintiff asked for?" It was over, we won. The jury awarded me $185,000 in proven damages plus costs. I ran out of the construction trailer jumping and yelling "we won, we won, WE WON". When I later talked to Strother he said that was the largest award for a discrimination case ever awarded in a United States Federal District Court at that time.

CHAPTER 32:

TIME IS NOT ON OUR SIDE

Months and months pass. Strother said it only takes 6 to 8 weeks to certify a jury trial. More than enough time had passed to file appeals. It was December when the ruling came down, nine months after the verdict came down. The judge ruled the jury had erred in its decision and overturned the case ruling in favor of Roanoke County. You must understand that the judge, Judge Dalton, was the son of former Governor of Virginia. The same governor who appointed most of the State Corporation Commissioners and seated judges. The same Governor who had close ties to Appalachian Power Company and was very popular with the prevailing business pulse of Virginia.

In the meanwhile, work was finished in Atlantic City and I needed to get another job. This time in it was in New York City working on the subway improvements. It was dirty work with dust and urine smells reeking from the end of the stations. Most of this work was done at night or weekends. I rented a place in Staten Island and sent home $900.00 per month for child support. I even bought Ginny a new compact Dodge and paid for her to go back to school to get a Master's Degree in Special Education. I had very little money left after taxes. I had met lots of other contractors whom admired my work and dedication.

One night at the 133rd street station we were getting ready to pour concrete the next day during regular hours. I was on a scaffold on my back making sure all the forms and reinforcing rods were in place and the columns were properly boxed in. This station was about 80 years old and when we broke out the concrete surrounding the columns we found that the orange lead paint was still wet after all those years. That was good protection as the columns were the only thing holding up the street above. There were many areas in the subway system where you could grab a metal column and it would disintegrate in your hand being heavily rusted over the years with the constant dampness in the tunnels.

Just then, a train pulled into the station and stopped while heading southbound in my direction. The flagman blew his whistle singling the train was ready to leave the station and all construction personnel were to get into a safe spot. I shimmied my body along the scaffolding against the roof of the tunnel directly above the tracks. Before I could catch my balance, I fell about 18 feet landing on the inside track and my right arm bounced off the wood covering the 3rd rail. The right side of me had hit the inside steel rail squarely on my right thigh. Then the train started to move towards me sounding it's horn. I couldn't move for a second, the pain was penetrating as I moved. Nobody saw me, not even a member of the construction crew as they had already moved out from the tracks. My right arm moving around and pushing on the cover over the 3rd rail. I was finally able to raise up my torso and the train engineer didn't see me even with my reflective vest on due to the angle I was lying on. A direction parallel to the ground and the vest wasn't reflecting light back to the train. The train kept coming, I pushed myself with my right arm above the 3rd rail and managed to flip over into the middle area where the polluted water drained and the train kept on coming. I was able to make one final leap over the third rail between columns separating the northbound and southbound tracks just a second or two before the subway train passed just were I was lying.

That was close, too close. When I hobbled home I got to look at the damage, a contusion about half the size of a Nerf football sliced down the middle popped up on my right calf. It really hurt, but luckily my back seemed to be alright. Even more amazing, I didn't hit the 3rd rail which was right there with my right hand. Once again fate was looking over me. I came so very close to dying then and there from two different causes, the train and electrocution.

CHAPTER 33:

THE FINAL TRY

S. Strother Smith III had filed an appeal with the Fourth Federal Court of Appeals in Richmond. They granted a hearing rather quickly. The appeal was scheduled for October 4, 1984. This wasn't a trial per se, but a procedural hearing as to whether the judge acted correctly in overturning the case. I don't remembering going to that hearing, I don't think I did. But, if I did or did not, the appeal took place. Three judges were seated to hear the arguments. Their decision came down quickly too, but wasn't finally published until August 8, 1985. They reversed Judge Dalton's ruling as inappropriate, we won again in a 2 to 1 decision with one dissenting vote. For some reason, I didn't get overjoyed with excitement. I didn't really feel anything.

The decision handed down by the Unites States Forth District Circuit Court of Appeals came down in 51 parts. I'm only going over a few as many have to do with points of law. These are taken from "Justia U.S. Law" publications which reviews all Supreme Court and U.S. Federal Appellate Courts rulings.

#4 "The county attorney testified that he could not remember being at the meeting... Clark said that he simply cautioned Whalen to make clear in testifying that his views were his own, not those of Roanoke County..." (These actions were actually from the meeting that occurred in February 1976 when the County Attorney was not present after the power company plotted out the lines and found the route of no route and Clark and the County Attorney deliberately forgot about the meeting of March 17, 1975).

#5 "Whalen again opposed Appalachian Power as a private citizen at a Commission hearing in 1977 after obtaining permission from his supervisor........Clark, by contrast, testified that he knew nothing of Whalen's second testimony." (That is correct, Mr. Clark knew nothing of the second testimony before the hearing. But, he definitely knew about it after the rate increase was denied.)

#7 "In March 1979, Clark fired Whalen because of his business relationship with a Roanoke real estate broker. Clark claimed that Whalen's status as a real estate agent registered in Roanoke under the broker conflicted with his official responsibilities to review Roanoke subdivision developments. Clark testified that when he first learned that Whalen was pursuing a real estate license, he understood that Whalen would conduct business in Floyd County alone... According to Clark, Whalen explained that he needed to be apprenticed with a Roanoke broker because he could not fulfill the real estate licensing requirement in Floyd County. Clark accepted Whalen's explanation and his pledge not to appear publicly as a Roanoke real estate agent to avoid an appearance of impropriety. Only later, Clark claimed, did he learn of Whalen's involvement in Roanoke County land transaction." (It was at this time that Mr. Clark presented me with the letter stating forth these conditions and there were no new transactions thereafter.)

#8 "Whalen's real estate activities elicited complaints from other Roanoke brokers, prompting Clark to send a letter to Whalen on January 30, 1979, that set out the purported earlier agreement and demanded Whalen to choose between a career in Roanoke real estate and continued employment with the county. Whalen wrote "I concur" on the letter. Clark testified that after he learned that Whalen had received a commission from a transaction concerning property in the county, he discharged him." (Mr. Clark knew about my transaction prior to the letter and that prompted him to write the letter. He did not send me the letter, he presented the letter to me in his office in front of him. We reached a verbal agreement as to my giving up my real estate license only as a possible impropriety to others observing from the outside and there were no further real estate transactions on my part.)

#11 "Two hours after returning to work, Clark fired him again, citing his "failure to properly discharge responsibilities on behalf of Roanoke County." According to Clark, Whalen improperly reduced a subdivision performance bond for property being developed by the Roanoke broker with whom Whalen had been associated. Clark claims he was informed of the bond problem by the new county engineer, Raymond Robertson, sometime after Whalen's grievance hearing. He directed Robertson to contact Guepe, Whalen's former superior, to make sure the bond was unauthorized, because only the County Engineer had authority to release security. Clark never confronted Whalen directly, testifying instead that he felt convinced contact with Guepe had been made. Robertson could not recall contacting Guepe, noting he felt contact was made." (Whom is kidding whom, none of these allegations were true, just everybody felt that it was that way.)

#12 "Documents before the jury established that the broker wrote Whalen on November 29, 1978, to seek release of over $32,000 held in a $40,000 letter of credit for the subdivision. Whalen responded on December 4, 1978, by partially denying the request, citing the amounts of security needed to ensure proper drainage, paving, and soil erosion control. Whalen's letter was checked by Guepe, released $24,000 in all."

#13 "Robertson testified the he was upset by Whalen's release in light of the condition of the subdivision's roads. Robertson considered partial releases of security to be an unwise policy. Even if a contractor met individual obligations that were assigned particular values during the calculation of the bond, Robertson preferred to hold all the bond until the whole job was done."

#15 "Guepe testified that he supervised bond reductions during his tenure as county engineer. He affirmed that Whalen's reduction letter appeared to be normal and customary." (I'm surprised Art didn't step up to the plate, but with a witch hunt going on it was probably better for him to step back from assuming to much responsibility.)

#21 "Tested by the principals governing motions for judgment notwithstanding the verdict and claims of first amendment, mixed motive retaliation, the evidence was sufficient to defeat the motion. The testimony Whalen gave before the State Corporation Commission regarding the location of a power line in Floyd County concerned a matter of public interest sufficiently important for the Commission to convene a public hearing. Whalen's right to comment on a matter of public concern outweighs Roanoke County's interest in promoting the efficiency of public service. The record discloses that Roanoke County had no interest in the location of the power line in Floyd County. Roanoke County does have an interest in assuring that its employees do not undertake to represent the county without authority. The evidence, however, does not establish that Whalen misrepresented the capacity in which he appeared before the Commission. In answer to a question from the official conducting the hearing about his occupation, he responded truthfully that he was an engineer employed by Roanoke County. He did not represent that he spoke on behalf of the county, nor does it appear that the Commission gained that impression. Consequently, Whalen's testimony before the Commission was protected by the first amendment."

#22 "We cannot accept Clark's argument that the judgment notwithstanding the verdict was justified because the evidence was insufficient to show causation. Whalen was obligated to establish causation by proving that his testimony before the Commission was a substantial or motivating factor in Clark's decision to fire him. We cannot question Whalen's credibility when reviewing the grant of the motion."

#23 "Most importantly, the evidence showed that Clark actually undertook to fire Whalen because of his testimony at the Commission hearing. Indeed, Clark would have fired Whalen had not the county attorney advised against it."

#24 "The evidence also discloses that after unsuccessfully attempting to fire Whalen because of his testimony, Clark fired him for reasons deemed unacceptable by a neutral grievance committee. Two hours after Whalen was reinstated, Clark summarily fired him ostensibly for a reason that Clark had known about for some time. The evidence does not disclose that Clark was hostile to Whalen before Whalen testified at the Commission hearing."

#25 "Also, we must reject Clark's argument that the evidence compels acceptance of his testimony and his ultimate discharge and because there were intervening events, there is no basis on which the jury could infer a retaliatory motive. This argument, however, overlooks Clark's attempt to fire Whalen immediately after Whalen testified in opposition to Appalachian's proposal. The three-year interval was simply a factor for the jury to take into consideration in weighing the evidence. It does not compel reversal as a matter of law."

#42 "...Clark's admission that he was contacted by a power company employee about Whalen's activities. Whalen's failure to receive some merit raises despite satisfactory and above average job performance ratings, followed by the June 19, 1979 termination, these were bare facts might have risen to the level of "probability" required under Mayberry, although to say so would require, I believe, that Mr. Clark possess a memory that even an elephant would envy..."

This is a quote from the dissenting judge. (Effectually, Clark became an unknowing pawn of the power company. A word or two here or there raising doubt in Mr. Clark's mind about an employee from a highly trusted source within the power company and has caused him to believe everything he was told or to question my activities against the power company. You need to make up your mind as to Mr. Clarks elephant like memory).

With the appeal won I went home to Virginia to visit the kids. Ginny actually wanted to have sex with me. We agreed to rent a summer rental for a couple for weeks in Ocean City, New Jersey close to where I was working and see how it went, maybe reconcile before the final divorce decree was entered. We rented the upper duplex unit 4 blocks from the ocean for the month of June. The owner gave me the keys for the week prior to Memorial Day weekend so I could crash there until my family came up.

CHAPTER 34:

PURGERY

Definition from Google: "The offense of willfully telling an untruth in a court after having taken an oath or Affirmation."

How do the attorneys for Appalachian Power Company overcome the truth and right of the plaintive. They got a highly respected person in the community with impeccable credentials to lie. Well, they had the perfect patsy, Mr. William F. Clark.

In the testimony, Mr. Clark had alluded to the meeting in February 1976 stating Mr. Ed Natt, county attorney was present. That certainly did occur, but without Mr. Natt. Both Mr. William F. Clark and Ed Natt had denied the existence of the March 17th, 1976 meeting when Mr. Clark so emphatically fired me. That meeting was so very hard to forget. They merely stated that they didn't recollect such a meeting, not that there was no such meeting knowing that if they had fully denied the meeting, it would have been an out and out lie. But forgetting such an important meeting in itself is still lying to the courts.

Now that Roanoke County was being represented by Appalachian Power Company's attorneys, they could not admit to that meeting on March 17, 1976 as it would completely shatter their case for dismissal. Did the Appalachian Power Company attorneys advise them not to disclose this meeting and lie about it on the witness stand under oath? Or was it a decision that both Mr. William F. Clark and Mr. Ed Natt conspired to perjure themselves on the witness stand? The problem with this is that the dissenting vote was specifically based upon the testimony of Mr. Clark that there was no such meeting. Once again citing from "Justia U.S. Law"

#48 "In addition to the overwhelming evidence of the problems produced by Whalen's real estate activities, I am also influenced by the absence of any proof that Clark ever discussed Whalen's Corporation Commission appearance after 1976, or that Appalachian Power Company either conspired with Clark or exerted any pressure upon him." By dissenting judge Ervin.

It is clear to me that lies were told in order to get conflicting testimony into the record which became their way out. The overturning of physical court appearances where a direct result to the conspiracy of Mr. Clark, Mr. Natt and Appalachia Power company attorneys to create confusion and a method to convince judges to overturn cases. All based on lies told under oath.

CHAPTER 35:

WORKING FOR THE ????

I got a call from Ginny. The case wasn't over yet. Roanoke County filed for a special hearing in full court to review the Appellate court's decision. It wasn't Roanoke County; it was the Appalachian Power Companies attorneys. I said I had faith in the system and knew a fair and just court would uphold the decision.

In the meanwhile I was approached by a construction manager and said they were hiring and I fit their needs perfectly. I was to be digging in the dirt out in the open away from dirty, filthy and smelly subways. The hours were good and the work was exciting. In downtown New York City you can't dig without major problems and my first assignment was the underpinning of a building near Washington Square, on 18th Street if I remember properly. Underpinning is where the new foundation is deeper than the older foundations and are directly attached to the new property. The new foundations went to bedrock and the building was to be much taller than the 10 to 15 story older buildings that didn't have foundations going all the way to bedrock.

My pay had jumped from $1,150 per week before taxes to $1,500 per week. A well needed bump in salary. However, on the first payday on the second Friday of my work there, a limo pulls up to the site and the man that hired me rolls down the window and introduces me to the Boss. I'll call him Fast Eddy. He handed me 15 one hundred dollar bills and said good work. All cash? No deductions. It turned out he was the mob boss for the west Brooklyn area. Well, I couldn't go back to my previous employer and the money was too good. I went from one job site to another, one was solid rock and we needed to blast. That is what every kid dreams of playing in the dirt, building things and blasting things up. Soon after that job things began to unravel.

Fast Eddy's office was located on a major road next to the Brooklyn elevated expressway on its way to the Verrazano Narrows Bridge. It was a full city block in size, but hollow in the center with a large courtyard in the middle. One day getting my pay while waiting in the hall Fast Eddy was talking to his attorney with the office door open. They were talking about the transfer deed to Fast Eddy and that there was a cloud over the title. The previous owner hadn't signed the deed before he mysteriously disappeared. A slight oversight in the mob world, but a good attorney could handle it. And to boot, there was no record of a transfer of the $600,000 plus sales price into the previous owners account. Did Fast Eddy have him erased?

Well, that was New York City for you, and it got better. Fast Eddy ran a garbage carting business. He undercut the competition and took only cash with no questions asked about the waste. That was a robust business in those days, plus he ran the construction business. One night the two were melded together when the city shut down one of my job sites on 3rd Avenue in midtown Manhattan. In order to get paid he needed to remove the remaining dirt from the site, but the city said no. All the underpinning rods were in place except for one that hit a pocked of soft rock and could not be anchored after two attempts the city shut the job down until it was completed. One night after midnight, Eddy had 6 of his monster roll off container trucks line up at the site and the clam bucket was used to dig out and fill up these 40 yard containers to overflowing, well over the legal limits. When each truck left I was amazed to see them flopping back and forth with tires squished way down as to look somewhat flat. The tarp over the mounded trucks was the only thing holding the rock and dirt mix in the container if it even held it. If a police car would have come by the site it would have been shut down and the operators carted off to jail. Police cars were always seen driving down this avenue all day long . I was there for about 3 full hours and not one police car drove by during this time, I wonder why? It was almost as if they were instructed not to go down 3rd Avenue.

The very next week I went to the Brooklyn office for my Friday pay. Now, at this time the city had placed an embargo on trash ships taking trash to another country to be dumped, and that was one of the ways Eddy got rid of his trash. The inside court of his building was about 200 by 200 and was filled 2 stories high in trash with a dozer parked on top. He was so awash with trash that he had about 20 containers filled with trash and construction debris rolled off and parked on the streets surrounding the building. Then I saw something even weirder. There were about 10 light brown city vehicles with little blue lights on top surrounding the building. I got into the building and went to the pay area where I was handed my envelope and a rifle.

Now let me tell you something, handing me a gun is like handing down a death warrant on someone. While stationed at Yuma Proving Grounds there was little to do after work. I took up pistol shooting. I got good enough to find a spot on the base pistol team. I only qualified as a NRA marksman, the lowest classification. The good part about being a member of this team we would go TDY, that's a per diem value to cover expenses paid while going to different shooting matches in San Diego, Phoenix and Las Vegas to shoot against the local police, Nettles Air Force Base in Las Vegas and other local pistol teams. I got to be quite proficient as shooting the 45 caliber hard ball pistol. Hard ball is the rounded run of the mill manufactured bullet while most competition shooters used 38 caliber wad cutter, less recoil and flat top that punched out a perfect hole instead of tearing the target paper.

While shooting at the Phoenix pistol range I qualified at the top rank of Master shooting all but 2 bulls eyes, and those were solid 9's. That was an unexpected jump over the other 2 categories in between. That was that, the captain of the team sat me out and said I was going to the Grand Nationals in Chicago later that year. I would shoot as a marksman, the lowest category as I needed to qualify twice as a master to get a higher ranking. I practiced and practiced every day. 100 rounds per day minimum. I got to be so good that all my shots were in a group the size of a quarter. That's with a 45 caliber hard ball. However, my dreams of the National Championship were dashed when orders shipped me to Heidelberg, Germany. They didn't have a pistol team there.

I took my pay but refused to take a rifle and a position along the front and side windows overlooking the New York City Garbage Police barricade. They had no guns but had container horses, tractors trying to pick up Fast Eddy's parked containers. They were only able to get up 1 container that I know of as their tractors were of a much lighter hauling grade. It turned out that Fast Eddy, who became a made man in the mob during my tenure there, had over 100 tickets outstanding for dumping garbage under the Brooklyn and Manhattan bridges and at the end of City Island to name a few of his favorite dumping sites. As far as Eddy was concerned that stuff just slid off the truck in an accident, the driver accidentally hit the wrong petal, or something. But he never cleaned it up. This was the cities one major push to enforce the codes of the city, but woefully unsuccessful. I took my pay, gave back the rifle and said I wasn't coming back. I didn't, I just walked away from the mob.

CHAPTER 36:

BACK IN RICHMOND, VIGINIA

A few more months passed before the full seating of the appellate court hearing. I sat in the gallery and listened to the arguments, which had nothing to do with the case, just banter between the presenting attorney and the court. I was wondering why they were even doing this. Arguments had been filed by both Strother and Appalachian Power Company attorneys. I got to read both. The argument from the power company was about an incident in California that has nothing to do with the kind of case I was involved with. Strother's argument cited more cases that were more closely connected to my situation.

A few weeks later I found out why Appalachian Power Company attorneys called for this hearing. The 4th U. S. District Appellate Court did the unthinkable that wrenched so hard at my heart. They overturned the detailed appeal in favor of Roanoke County. I guess it wouldn't have been so bad if the decision came down 7 to 6 against me, or even 8 to 5. But no, the 13 judges came down 11 to 2 against me. That meant that the 10 new judges, all of whom knew little about this case, voted against me. Why would all of these 10 judges that had nothing to do with the appeal vote totally against me. They were sending a message loud and clear, don't mess with Appalachian

Power Company. It was the good old boys against a country bumpkin.

I called Strother. He told me that I had 6 months to get together $50,000 up front in cash to post with the United States Supreme Court if I wanted to proceed any further. And that was just the first installment, more would be needed and that didn't guarantee the Supreme Court would even hear the case. At that time I was in between jobs and had no money saved up and Ginny had none either.

Half the money I took home went for child support and the other half just covered my expenses while living in Staten Island, New York, then later to southern New Jersey. I couldn't go any further. They won and I lost everything I had other than the new life I had started. I never returned to Virginia except passing thru on I-95. There is a pain that resonates throughout my body, the embarrassment that accompanies total defeat having to walk away from everything you loved. All my old friends really didn't know the truth about what was happening or had happened. The only things they knew is what they heard from the news and press releases. We didn't speak of these matters, maybe they thought the lesser of me and they didn't want to embarrass me. I left behind my home and the land of which I had become so attached to. I loved it here, the people, the way of life, the respect, and Virginia Tech from where I got my inner strength. I only saw my kids a few times the next couple of summer afterwards, but they stopped coming to see me. But my memories are fading with time, least they should ever leave me. Love knows no bounds, no season and never dies. Just don't look back.

I now know that from the time the Appalachian Power Company Attorneys took over at the first trial, they won. Even if they lost, they won. They were in with the courts and their power was absolute regardless if they were right or wrong. The outcome was sealed. If the power company attorneys had won the first trial at Federal District Circuit Court, it would have ended there. It didn't as we had won. But, they had time and extreme influence on their side. That was evidenced by the fact that they didn't request an appeal of the lower court decision. They knew that the power they wielded would come around in their favor, probably from the very first day after the verdict. They had time on their side. When we won the appeal, they still won knowing that their influence would be on their side at the full attendance review by the appellate court judges. Then, shear economics was on their side and a low probability of this case ever being heard by the Supreme Court. Why did the power company take over the legal fight for Roanoke County Board of Supervisors to begin with? It wasn't because they didn't have attorneys working for them. No, the had two. Not that they couldn't hire other attorneys well qualified to defend the honor of Roanoke County. No, the Appalachian Power Company and American Electric Power had a $144,000,000 per year bone to pick with me. Letting a one-man engineering and economic team flying sold without any additional outside help defeat them at their own game. This was unheard of and they wanted revenge.

There is a lot to be said about burning your bridges behind you. The further away I was from it, the less it hurt. Only a single radio newsman followed my side of the story at the beginning. The day he released his side in those early days, he never spoke to me again. I wonder why?

I was crushed, my faith in the government crumbled beneath me like a pillar of sand collapsing as the Federal Court system had been breached. My faith in those in high positions disappeared. My faith in god was compromised as I became a divorced catholic. The farm was divided and sold off. There was nothing left here for me. Roanoke; the star city of the south with the white star shining over the city just became tarnished. Since the divorce was finalized, I haven't returned to Roanoke.

CHAPTER 37:

THE AFTERMATH

Soon afterwards, I believe in 1985, I was driving home from work getting ready to cross the bridge to Staten Island listening to the news. The business section came up and I was surprised to hear American Electric Power Company made a public announcement that it was halting its massive power line and generating plant construction program. Citing the area was not growing at the rate it had projected from the 1978 State Corporation Commission hearing that I had been a part of. I have never been against the construction of power lines and power plants as needed, just the wasteful spending of the consumers money for power lines not needed. I didn't oppose the Appalachian Power Company proposal to build a line from the Martinsville substation tying into Carolina Power and Light's 500 Kva power line and connecting with the existing 765 Kva power line. I just found a far better way for them to do it without harming new areas. Without the $144,000,000 per year increase for construction, they couldn't afford to build it on their own as it produced no new source power or revenue. Therefore, it was prudent to stop the expansive construction program of new 765 Kva power lines. Pure economics at work.

I can only imagine the massive amount of unneeded construction that would have followed should Appalachian Power Company have been awarded the funds from the rate increase hearing. Citizens of western Virginia and West Virginia would still be paying to this day for excess construction if I were not to have opposed the filling for rate increase. Over the 20 years of proposed construction presented to the State Corporation Commission, Appalachian Power Company would have collected $2,880,000,000 in new fees from its customers in Virginia alone. Of that $201,600,000 would have been tax free A.F.U.D.C. money had the State Corporation Commission of Virginia allowed the rate increase.

But this was too late for the good people of Floyd County as the southern leg requested by Appalachian Power Company was completed prior to this announcement. That was the one leg that I had contended should not have been built at all. That a much shorter leg with virtually no new environmental degradation was available adjacent to the existing power line corridor between Roanoke and Martinsville, VA. That was the only new 765 Kva power line built by American Electric Power Company to that date.

Art Guepe had resigned from his position on May 11, 1979. I had the opportunity of contacting Art and forwarding him an early copy of this manuscript. He found it to be "factual to my (his) recollection." As of August 20, 2012, Art refused to put any comments in writing.

Later, I made an attempt to contact Mr. Edward Natt, but found out that he passed away in December of 2009.

I also contacted S. Strother Smith 9/5/2012 and sent him a copy.

A few years ago, my son from my 2nd marriage just turned 18 and being the big help he thinks he is, did something extraordinary, well not him. Leaving the office on a second story office building one breezy day, I gave my son a handful of papers to hold while I went to the bathroom. He went to the car and stood outside having a cigarette while I went to the potty. I was sitting behind metal partitions, in a masonry block walled bathroom with no windows, on the second floor. I saw my son. It was as if a drop down window appeared in the front of my forehead. I saw my son running thru the parking lot after pages of the papers that I gave him. When I finally got down to the parking lot, he was standing next to the car with papers in hand. I asked him if he got them all. "Yeah" he responded and asked me how I knew. I told him "I saw you running after them". I even went in the direction he went and motioned in the similar manor as he did. He agreed that was what he did. "Yes!" I said, "I still have it". Whatever it is, I really don't know what it is; but it's real and I still have it!

CHAPTER 38:

TIME CHANGES THINGS

I ended up meeting and marrying a bright eyed girl that I met around the end of this story. She gave me more love than I could ever have imagined. But, more than that she filled the emptiness in my heart from the loss of my family, friends and livelihood that surely would have consumed me if it were not for her. I had promised her that I would put this whole incident behind me and not write about these things for fear of some reprisals and personal incriminations against both of us. But, now that almost 30 years have passed, there is no fear from actions in the past now behind us being held against us.

Over the winter of 2012 I had my first heart attack. I began to think that I could die at any moment. If so, they would have gotten off free and clear of all their misconduct. Nobody would know what I endured, so I started writing that winter, and I wrote, and wrote. The difficulty was not remembering as this was imprinted deeply into my inner fabric, it was the separating of emotions that kept on coming up. Every person and place that I loved had been erased from my life and the reliving of them kept bringing tears to my eyes. Sometimes laughter, but mostly remorse of what could have been, and my children that I lost contact with.

I had never seen the 4th District Court of Appeals decision until July, 2012. I was amazed by the results and found out that the whole reversal was based on a calculated lie. I had exhausted my efforts fighting a system that was pro big business and government. That was acceptable in the 1980's. But since so much time has passed and the judges that went along with the big political machinery are no longer in the position of power to make biased judgments. This I truly wish has happened, but you never know. Thus this story can now be written without those suppressors of truth while greed and mighty corporations are flaunting the laws of the land with their power. Hopefully the tide has changed the jaded thinking of the 2nd most highest court in our land over the years and this will never happen again.

Looking back upon there events I can only imagine the pressure placed upon Mr. Clark to Win. In his position as chief administrator of all employees of Roanoke County he was probably presented with an ultimatum to win or lose his job as he could no longer be the man in charge with losing a civil rights violation case against him. Nor would he be able to find gainful employment anywhere in charge of employees.

There is a high probability that Mr. Clark went back to his buddies at Appalachian Power Company and requested their help as they were the ones that started this whole mess to begin with. If this happened, Appalachian Power Company would have offered their best trial lawyers for free to defend Mr. Clark so he could keep his position as top administrator for Roanoke County. And this is exactly what happened, they defended Mr. Clark, Roanoke County and got revenge against me at the same time. 2 for the price of 1 so to say.

CHAPTER 39:

MISCONDUCT

Roanoke County is responsible to the citizens it serves. It must live by a higher standard attempting to provide excellence in its dealings with the public from which it derives its authority. On the other hand, Appalachian Power Company has a duty to provide high quality continuous power to its customers in the western portion of Virginia. But reports to the stockholders, in this case American Electric Power Company.

If the 4th Circuit Court would have certified the original jury, there is a high probability that Roanoke County would have accepted the results with no further action. For Roanoke County to become the aggressor after losing the case and going to the Appellate Court would have looked vindictive and only exacerbated the wounds in the public's eye. Therefore, the Judge had to make a miraculous intervention in the County's favor with excess lobbying behind the scenes by Mr. William F. Clark and the Attorneys from Appalachian Power Company to have the judge throw out the verdict and by holding on to the original trial not needing to have a new trial with "new evidence." The Judge didn't allow it in to his good judgment as there probably would not have been a different outcome. But, what the Judge did do was to reverse the outcome of the trial in favor of Roanoke County, Mr. William F. Clark and Appalachian Power Company with a seldom used technicality.

The same holds true at the 4th U. S. Circuit Court of Appeals in Richmond. After winning the appeal, if Roanoke County would have pressed on to the Supreme Court they again would look vindictive against me, but on a national level. Thus, additional finagling by the Attorneys was needed to keep the pressure on me to be the one fighting the losing battles. Why the courts couldn't let the case run a normal course is because of political and corporate intervention to change positions and the outcome making the wrongdoer look innocent in the eyes of the public. It is seen that Woods - Rogers did influence the outcome of the trial and all subsequent actions in their favor. And why did the courts allow these actions? Was it because of undue familiarity? The wheels of justice are large and cumbersome. The road through which justice must travel is straight, long and narrow. Getting them to switch directions so quickly would have taken a lot of grease under the wheels. I wasn't privileged to these behind the scenes actions and can only imagine the pressure put upon the courts to continually reverse judgments by a competent jury and by prudent Appellate Court hearing.

Once again, UT PROSIM. Did I live up to that daunting level of expectation? Did I serve my fellow community unerringly? Or did I make a big mistake? Only you can decide that.

THE END.

www.ingramcontent.com/pod-product-compliance
Lightning Source LLC
Chambersburg PA
CBHW071000120626
46546CB00003B/864